103rd U.S. Open Championship
Olympia Fields Country Club
June 12-15, 2003

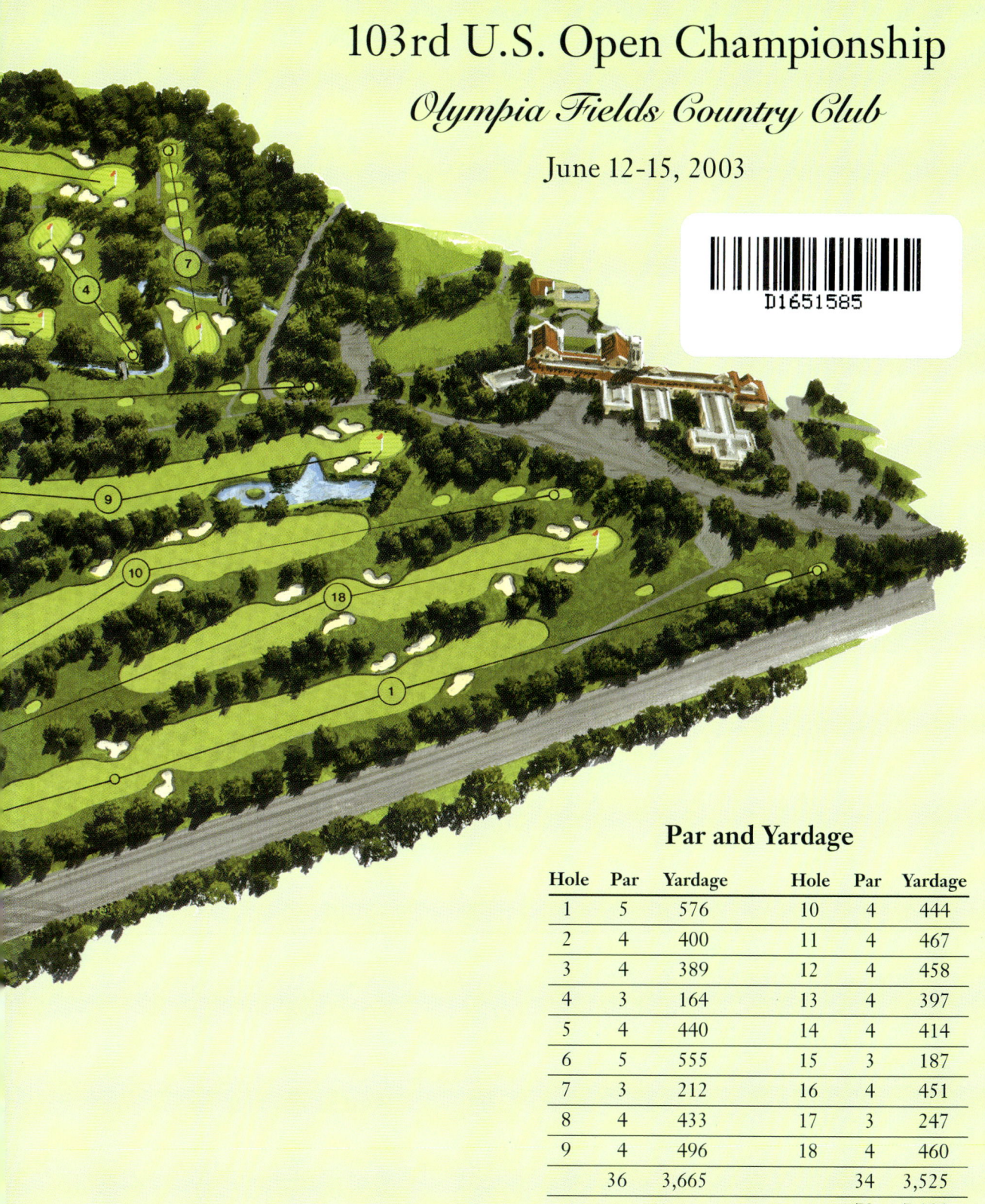

Par and Yardage

Hole	Par	Yardage	Hole	Par	Yardage
1	5	576	10	4	444
2	4	400	11	4	467
3	4	389	12	4	458
4	3	164	13	4	397
5	4	440	14	4	414
6	5	555	15	3	187
7	3	212	16	4	451
8	4	433	17	3	247
9	4	496	18	4	460
	36	3,665		34	3,525
				70	7,190

103rd U.S. OPEN
Olympia Fields Country Club

Writer: Robert Sommers   Photographers: Michael Cohen, Phil Inglis   Editor: Bev Norwood

ISBN 1-878843-38-9

©2003 United States Golf Association®
Golf House, Far Hills, N.J. 07931

Statistics produced by Unisys Corporation

Photograph on page 5 courtesy of Golf Magazine Custom Publishing
Photograph on page 7 courtesy of Jim and Mort Olman (Arthur Weaver, artist)
Course photography by Stephen Szurlej
Course illustrations by Dan Wardlaw © The Majors of Golf

Published by IMG Worldwide Inc.,
1360 East Ninth Street, Cleveland, Ohio 44114

Designed and produced by Davis Design

Printed in the United States of America

Jim Furyk's solid victory in the 2003 United States Open Championship did not surprise anybody close to golf on the professional tour level. Even though it was his first major championship, Furyk had clearly established himself as one of the game's finest players in recent years. After all, he had won seven tournaments before Olympia Fields and had been such a consistent player in recent years that he qualified for the last three Ryder Cup and the last two Presidents Cup teams and had won more than $13 million in his career.

I admired the way Jim handled his position atop the leaderboard through the weekend, when we have seen so many leaders of the Open succumb to the pressure and fall back. Jim never seemed to lose his focus on the job at hand or be ruffled by anything going on around him.

He really was in a class by himself Saturday and Sunday. His steady play kept everyone else at bay — and I can assure you that it's a comforting luxury when you can drink in the applause as you approach the 72nd green with a four-stroke lead. Too bad he missed his par putt there that would have given him the all-time, 72-hole scoring record in the Open. He earned it.

Overall, Olympia Fields proved to be a more-than-adequate Open venue, particularly on the weekend when the sun and wind dried it out and made the greens much more challenging.

I am pleased, on behalf of Rolex and the USGA, to introduce this 19th annual publication that presents in impressive words and pictures the story of the U.S. Open Championship.

Arnold Palmer

103rd U.S. OPEN
Olympia Fields Country Club

Machine Gun Jack McGurn, chief assassin for the Al Capone mob in 1920s Chicago, played a fair game of golf. As the ex-officio "professional" at the Evergreen Golf Club, a notorious mob hangout, he is known to have played in public at least once — at Olympia Fields Country Club during the 1933 Western Open. Seventy years later, in June of 2003, the cream of international golf gathered at Olympia Fields for the 103rd United States Open Championship. McGurn did not play: He died in 1936 as he had lived — gunned down by rival killers.

The world had changed since those days of bootleg whiskey and open warfare among mobs shooting it out on city streets. At the time of the 1933 Western Open, McGurn ranked No. 5 on the FBI's Public Enemy list, suspected of at least 25 murders and for plotting the St. Valentine's Day massacre, among the most brazen episodes in criminal history.

He faced prosecution only once, after Capone mobsters mowed down seven members of the Bugsy Moran gang in a Chicago garage on February 14, 1929, a crime so blatant it attracted nationwide attention and, perversely, glamorized Capone.

A jury acquitted McGurn when Louise Rolfe, a blonde showgirl, swore in court that she and McGurn had spent the day together in her hotel room. Police learned she had lied, but when the state threatened to try her for perjury, he married her to block her testimony. She became known as the blonde alibi.

By 1933, with Capone in prison, convicted of income tax evasion, McGurn had lost most of his influence, but law enforcement officials still considered him so dangerous that municipal judge Thomas Green issued a warrant for his arrest under a new "criminal reputation" law. The hunt was on, but where to find him?

Machine Gun Jack McGurn and his wife Louise.

Unluckily for McGurn, Joseph Shoemaker, Chicago's chief of detectives, read the sports pages. Browsing through first-round scores of the Western Open the morning of Aug. 26, he spotted, among the Tommy Armours, the Macdonald Smiths and the Jock Hutchisons, the name Vince Gebardi, which may or may not have been McGurn's real name. (Different sources claim different names, ranging from James DeMora or Jack Demore, to Vincenzo Gibaldi. Five Chicago newspapers used five different spellings of Gebardi.)

Whatever the spelling, it was close enough for Chief Shoemaker. He sent detective sergeants John Griffith and John Warren to arrest McGurn, and they in turn reflected on his delicate temper and recruited an armed backup force of Lieutenant Frank McGillen and five uniformed policemen from the county highway patrol.

It was a shame in a way because McGurn had recovered from his shaky 83 of the first day and

The 10th hole, par 4 and 444 yards.

shaved one stroke from par through six holes of the second round. When the gendarmes first spotted him strutting down the seventh fairway, they saw a confident, deeply tanned golfer immaculately clad in well-creased gray flannel slacks, white shirt, a yellow tie with red dots and black-and-white winged-tip shoes. They stood quietly as he played a nice approach to the green, then moved in and placed him under arrest.

Walter Fitzmaurice, a reporter for the *Chicago Tribune*, described the scene in the paper's Aug. 27 edition:

> McGurn was matched with Howard Holtman, a quiet young man from Beecher, Ill., who was unaware of Gebardi's identity.
>
> McGurn's wife … was trailing along to encourage him, flashing on one hand a three-carat diamond ring and on the other a glittering wedding band.
>
> The officers surveyed the scene with professional eyes, noting especially the presence of Louise, who was clad in a tight white dress, white hat and anklet stockings. She, too, was heavily tanned, having played in a women's tournament over the same course a few weeks ago.
>
> "The heat must be off between the mobs or McGurn wouldn't bring her here," mused Lieutenant McGillen. "If the Touhys were after him, they could shoot both him and his wife with a rifle like sparrows from here."
>
> The players approached the seventh green. The lieutenant advanced and read the warrant. The gangster's partner caught the name Machine Gun Jack McGurn but didn't flinch. McGurn, too, seemed cool enough. He heard the lieutenant out in silence, then civily asked permission to finish the game and resumed his play. He took a 6 at the hole, two over par.
>
> They'd hardly begun the eighth hole when Louise tore into the cops.
>
> "Who's bright idea was this?" she barked at McGillen. The lieutenant shrugged.
>
> Then a photographer dashed up to McGurn and snapped three pictures. Visibly upset, McGurn's lips tightened, his hands trembled and his game collapsed. He played the hole in 11 strokes, dropping seven strokes on one hole.
>
> Enraged now, McGurn turned to the photographer, grabbed him by the shirt and shook him, snarled and snapped, "You've ruined my game."

Not totally. Even though he had lost nine strokes to par on two holes, he still shot 86, which wasn't bad.

Nevertheless, off to jail he went. But not satisfied with permission to finish the round, McGurn asked to drive himself to the lockup. Once again the police agreed, so off they drove in the culprit's roadster, McGurn and Louise up front, and the two detectives in the rumble seat. Word is they arrived safely and promptly — every last one.

Macdonald Smith won that Western Open, beating a field made up of, in addition to Armour and Hutchison, perennial contenders Ralph Guldahl, Harry Cooper, Leo Diegel, Horton Smith, Johnny Revolta, the great amateur Chick Evans and a pair of 21-year-old Texans just making their way in professional golf. Byron Nelson, a few months the older, shot 295 and tied for seventh, but after opening with a good 73, Ben Hogan slipped to 84 in the second round and missed the cut by two strokes.

Olympia Fields spread over nearly 700 acres in those days, covered by four golf courses, a polo field, riding trails, trap and skeet shooting and archery ranges, a lawn bowling pitch, skating rink, a 30-by-15-yard pool with depths ranging from three feet to 11 feet that could accommodate 300 swimmers, and indoor facilities for table tennis, tenpin bowling, cards and other table games.

So vast was the clubhouse, members claimed that if ever it could be straightened, none but the strongest drives would reach from one end to the other.

It was indeed immense. The building and its grounds spread over more than five acres, took two years to build and cost $1.3 million. More than 1,300 members and guests attended the inaugural banquet and danced to three bands.

Its dining room could seat 800 and its grill room another 600. It had a dance pavilion, a sort of hotel for members (along with a bellman), what it called its own hospital, which amounted to a nurse on regular duty, a barber shop, beauty salon, an ice-making plant and a group of members who declared themselves the club's volunteer fire department.

Like Pine Valley, Olympia Fields became an incorporated village.

The club had been founded in 1913 by Charles M. Beach, a visionary who dealt in real estate. With golf spreading through the region — Chicago Golf Club had opened in 1892, followed a few years later by Glen View, Onwentsia, Midlothian and Flossmoor — Beach determined to organize a club as well. Each morning he took the Illinois Central railroad 20 miles southward to the village of Flossmoor, then hiked southeasterly, searching for the perfect setting. After two days of scrabbling alone through cornfields, climbing hills, wading creeks and easing gingerly over barbed-wire fences, Beach persuaded his friend James P. Gardner to join him. Together they found what both men believed they could develop into more than one golf course, a plot of rolling land crossed by a placid stream lined by shade trees. It seemed ideal.

Opening a membership campaign, Beach and Gardner recruited Amos Alonzo Stagg as the club's first president. A pioneer coach whose University of Chicago teams ranked among the best in college football, Stagg hardly ever played golf, but his name attracted members. By July 1916 the club had a charter, and by February 1917, it had bought the land for $350 an acre.

The club set up shop in an old farmhouse and laid out a golf course before the last corn crop had been harvested. The second course had been built by the fall, a third by 1921 and the fourth, the gem of them all, by 1922.

Tom Bendelow designed the first and second courses, Willie Watson the third, and Willie Park Jr., the fourth. An able golfer and religious

Willie Park Jr. brought new ideas to Olympia Fields.

zealot, Bendelow laid out 650 courses over his long career, often taking no longer than an afternoon. He would drive one stake in the ground for a tee, another for a green, and leave the construction to others — common at the time.

All three of them Scots, Bendelow and Watson settled in the United States, but Park made his home in Scotland, although he spent extended periods in the United States. As an architect, he outshone them both — not in Bendelow's quantity, of course, but certainly in his quality. He ranked at the top of his craft.

The son of Willie Park, the first British Open champion and great rival of Old Tom Morris (both men won four British Opens), Willie Jr. won two of his own, his first in 1887 and his second two years later. His influence, though, reached beyond cham-

Olympia Fields Country Club

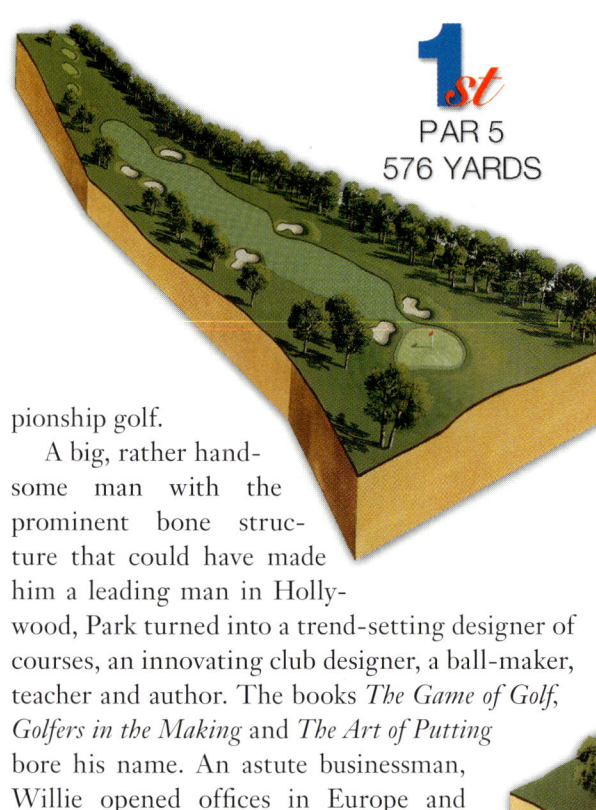

1st
PAR 5
576 YARDS

pionship golf.

A big, rather handsome man with the prominent bone structure that could have made him a leading man in Hollywood, Park turned into a trend-setting designer of courses, an innovating club designer, a ball-maker, teacher and author. The books *The Game of Golf*, *Golfers in the Making* and *The Art of Putting* bore his name. An astute businessman, Willie opened offices in Europe and the United States as his design business expanded, and he dabbled in real estate.

Born in 1864 into a family of golfers — his uncle, Mungo Park, won a British Open as well — Park grew up in Musselburgh, a small, grim town a few miles east of Edinburgh, where most of the better golfers assembled for money matches. Competing in that crowd, Willie Jr. found a way to hold his own. Through eternal practice, he developed into a deadly putter, convinced that, "a man who can putt is a match for anyone," an aphorism he claimed he conceived in 1890. Park lived up to it.

Using an unconventional putter of his own design that featured an offset blade, he made up two strokes over the last three holes at Musselburgh and beat Andrew Kirkaldy for the 1889 British Open. Two years earlier he had beaten Bob Martin at Prestwick.

Park broke with tradition in course design as well. Most bunkers of the period were nothing more than holes in the ground. Park introduced what the golf course architect Geoffrey Cornish calls capes — tongues of grass jutting into the sand — and bays — sweeping expanses of sand creeping up the forward slopes, as on the

2nd
PAR 4
400 YARDS

windswept links of Britain. He had followed this technique at Sunningdale, a wonderful course south of London, and introduced the concept at Olympia Fields.

Chicago sits on the great midwestern prairie, an expanse of generally level ground covered for eons by high grass tall as a man until European settlers pushed westward, plowed the grass under and turned grassland into farmland. Olympia Fields lies on just such gently rolling land with just a few noticeable grades. Park called the land the most perfect golf terrain he had ever seen and set to work weaving his holes through oak, maple, hawthorn, cherry, ash and enough other tree varieties to stock an arboretum. Taking advantage of its possi-

3rd
PAR 4
389 YARDS

The third hole, par 4 and 389 yards.

bilities, he brought the stream into play on half the holes. When he finished, Park considered Olympia Fields No. 4 his masterpiece, "The equal of any I have seen."

He finished in 1923, returned home to Scotland and died in 1925.

While Park's name is forever linked to No. 4, developments over the years in equipment, in agronomy, in maintenance practices, and the growing number of first-class golfers led to significant changes. The holes no longer play in the sequence Park designed, holes have been lengthened, greens rebuilt, principally to add hole locations, the trees have grown and some others have been cut down.

The club itself has changed as well. Olympia Fields hadn't been around more than 10 years when the Great Depression of the 1930s struck, putting a financial strain on the members. The club cut back on the dining room and grill, but hung on to its four courses. No. 4 began drawing the important championships.

First, in 1925 Walter Hagen won the second of his unmatched record of four consecutive PGA Championships, and three years later Johnny Farrell beat Bob Jones over 36 playoff holes for the 1928 United States Open.

Each championship had been distinctive in its own way. In the book *The Walter Hagen Story*, Hagen told of the day he arrived at Olympia Fields for the PGA Championship.

If you care to believe it, after overhearing Tommy Armour, Leo Diegel, Al Watrous, Bill Mehlhorn, Mike Brady and Harry Coo-

4th
PAR 3
164 YARDS

5th PAR 4 440 YARDS

6th PAR 5 555 YARDS

7th PAR 3 212 YARDS

per stage a mock argument over who among them would beat him, Hagen poked his head around the lockers, pointed to each in turn, and said slowly, "I wonder which one of you will be second?"

As good as his word, Hagen beat Watrous in the first round, Brady in the second, Diegel in the third, Cooper in the semi-finals and Melhorn in the final.

He won again the next two years, but his streak ended in 1928 at Five Farms, in Baltimore, where Diegel beat him in the third round. By then Hagen had lost the trophy; the PGA had to buy a new one.

Three years later the United States Golf Association took the Open to Olympia Fields, where once again a championship ended dramatically. With two holes to play, Roland Hancock, a 21-year-old North Carolinian, led by two strokes and had only to play the last two holes in no worse than two over par to beat Jones and Farrell by one stroke.

To reach the 17th tee, Hancock crossed the creek, reeking with overflow from bootleggers' stills upstream that flowed past a herd of contented cows before purling through Olympia Fields.

Whether it was the powerful vapors of the stream or the premature warning of a spectator who yelled, "Make way for the new champion," that caused it, Hancock butchered the closing holes. He took a 6 at the par-4 17th by playing a horrible shot from a bare patch in the rough, and closed with another 6 at the last, a par 5. With 295, he slipped to third place, a stroke behind Farrell and Jones.

The next day, Farrell stunned Jones by running off four consecutive birdies on the closing holes of the morning 18 and went to lunch three strokes ahead. Jones caught him early in the afternoon round, but Farrell moved ahead when Jones bogeyed the 16th and held on to the end. In a

memorable finish, both men birdied the 18th, a shortish par 5 of 490 yards.

By winning, Farrell became the last man to beat Jones in an Open. Jones won in 1929 and 1930, then retired from competition.

With the 1928 championship, Chicago had seen eight of the first 32 U.S. Opens. The city deserved them; it had been a seat of golf for many years.

Charles Blair Macdonald probably started it all. He had developed a passion for the game as a student at St. Andrews University, where he

103rd U.S. Open

The seventh hole, par 3 and 212 yards.

Olympia Fields Country Club

The ninth hole, par 4 and 496 yards.

hung around Old Tom Morris's shop and mingled with the great players of the late 19th century. Returning to Chicago, he missed the game so badly he laid out a few rough holes at Fort Douglas, an old Civil War encampment, and tried to stir interest among his friends.

Eventually, Macdonald founded the Chicago Golf Club, first laying out a seven-hole course at Lake Forest, then a nine-hole course at Belmont, in Chicago's western suburbs, then later another nine holes at Wheaton, a bit farther west. With more land at Wheaton, Macdonald added nine more within a year, creating what may have been the nation's first 18-hole course. It stands today without significant alteration.

Macdonald shares responsibility for the USGA as well. Under his prodding, the Chicago Golf Club joined with four other clubs and founded the association at a dinner meeting in New York late in 1894. The USGA conducted its first Open, Amateur and Women's Amateur championships the following year.

His support and influence won his Chicago Golf Club three of the first 17 U.S. Opens. Joe Lloyd won the 1897 Open, Harry Vardon won in 1900, and in 1911, Johnny McDermott became not only the first U.S.-born champion, but, at 19, the youngest.

Times had changed after 1928, and Chicago had seen only four Opens since the Farrell-Jones playoff, the last three at Medinah Country Club,

8th
PAR 4
433 YARDS

just west of O'Hare International Airport, in the northwestern suburbs. Cary Middlecoff had won at Medinah in 1949, Lou Graham in 1975 and Hale Irwin in 1990. Then in 2003 it returned to Olympia Fields.

The Olympia Fields that Hagen and Jones played in the 1920s was not the same for the 2003 Open. Even the course name had changed. Deeply in debt by 1944, first from the Great Depression and later from lack of patronage during the Second World War, the club sold most of Nos. 2 and 3 to home builders, who turned the land into a middle-class neighborhood. What had been No. 4 became the North Course, and remnants of Nos. 1 and 3 were blended into the South Course.

It was over the North Course that Jerry Barber, a bantam-like 5-foot-5 with a controlled fade and flawless putting stroke, beat Don January, a tall and lanky Texan, for the 1961 PGA Championship.

9th
PAR 4
496 YARDS

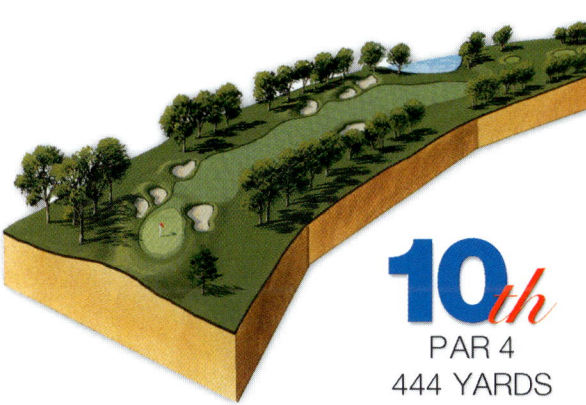

10th
PAR 4
444 YARDS

Among the game's shorter hitters, Barber made up for it with his uncanny putting. He beat January by first holing a series of long putts to catch up in the last round, then with a remarkable recovery from a fairway bunker the next afternoon that won the playoff.

Four strokes behind with three holes to play in the fourth round, Barber holed from 20 feet at the 16th, from 40 feet at the 17th, and from 60 feet at the 18th to pull even and force another 18 holes. The next day he made every putt he looked at again. Two strokes behind once more with seven to play, Barber dropped putts from 16 feet at the 12th, from 18 feet at the 14th and from 10 feet at the 15th. Behind by one, January birdied the 16th to pull even, but in the gathering gloom, Barber ripped a 3-iron from a fairway bunker within 18 feet at the last and two-putted for a change. It was good enough, because January bogeyed.

Barber and January shot 277 over a course that measured 6,725 yards, 31 yards shorter than the club's stated length 33 years earlier, when Jones and Farrell tied at 294.

While the sequence of holes had been changed for the 1961 PGA Championship, not only had the holes been switched once again for 2003, but early in the 1990s the course had been practically rebuilt.

11th
PAR 4
467 YARDS

13

Olympia Fields Country Club

12th
PAR 4
458 YARDS

Understanding the North Course had aged and must be strengthened to attract the big events, Olympia Fields brought in Mark Mungeam, a partner with Geoffrey Cornish and Brian Silva, to revise and restore it closer to Park's original concept. A specialist in restoration projects, Mungeam reshaped every bunker, rebuilt two greens and added 11 new tees, some in places no one had seen since Sitting Bull roamed the prairie. The new Olympia Fields measured 7,190 yards.

The Open field had no fear of the added yardage. After all, as long ago as 1965, Bellerive Country Club, in St. Louis, reached 7,191 yards, and like Olympia Fields, it played to a par of 70. If they felt intimidated at all, the field could blame the new, deeper bunkers and quick, slanting greens.

Nevertheless, Mungeam had indeed created a man-sized course. As it was set up for the Open, it began with a 576-yard par 5, and along the way threw in a 496-yard par 4 and a 247-yard par 3. Three other par 4s measured from 458 to 467 yards, and another par 3 stretched beyond 200 yards. In an unusual twist, both its par-5 holes fell within the first six holes; it finished with nine par 4s and three par 3s.

Yet in this age of three-piece balls that fly farther and metal-headed drivers that hit the ball straighter, extreme distances mean less than in years past. For example, Angel Cabrera played the ninth, the 496-yard par 4, by ripping his drive 360 yards and playing his approach with a lob wedge. And the field reached the sixth, the 555-yard par 5, routinely with the second shot.

Not length but terrain caused most problems for the field. A steep valley cut across both the fifth and 12th holes, a pair of par 4s that, in order, measured 440 yards and 458 yards. The 12th ranked as the most difficult Olympia Fields offered, and the

13th
PAR 4
397 YARDS

fifth was the third most difficult.

With their greens set high above the drive zones, approach shots that fell short risked rolling back down the hill and perhaps into Butterfield Creek, the stream that purls through the course.

Most players overclubbed, aiming for the rear of both greens, but with the Open at stake, Jim Furyk left his second shot barely on the front of the 12th green. That wasn't good enough. The ball rolled slowly off the green, gradually picked up speed, tumbled ever faster down the hill and stopped just short of the creek. He bogeyed, stalling his drive for the Open's 72-hole record of 272. (He tied it.)

The closing three holes tested everyone — a 451-yard par 4, the 247-yard par 3, and a 460-yard par 4. Many in the Open field played iron clubs to

14th
PAR 4
414 YARDS

The 15th hole, par 3 and 187 yards.

the 17th, but they didn't always reach the green.

Of all the revisions, only the deeper bunkers caused Mungeam anxiety. Nevertheless, it seemed necessary, particularly after the 1997 U.S. Senior Open, Olympia Fields's first USGA competition since the 1928 Open. Misdirected tee shots headed for trouble in fairway bunkers routinely skipped through the sand and bounced back into play. Something had to be done for the Open, but because Olympia Fields sits on a flood plain with a shallow water table, crews could dig down only a foot or two. Improvising, they scooped out perhaps two feet of sand and piled it above the bunker face, which, in effect, created a four-foot wall. Now fairway bunker shots demanded more lofted clubs, and the faces of some greenside bunkers rose so high, not everyone could see over them to the greens. Adding to the misery, the bunkers seemed to gobble up every ball that dropped nearby.

Deep bunkers can be handled, but

Olympia Fields Country Club

16th PAR 4 451 YARDS

Thorough though the planning may have been, a cold and wet spring stunted growth until shortly before the Open began on June 12. The rough wasn't as severe as everyone thought it would be, and spring rains left the greens soft and receptive to approach shots. Early rounds demonstrated how vulnerable even the strongest courses could be to the modern golfer. Not until two days of sunshine along with a breeze that swept through the course did Olympia Fields play as officials had hoped. With the greens firm and a moderate wind, scores climbed, leading to speculation on how high the winning total might have been under normal weather conditions.

the Olympia Fields greens caused more severe dilemmas. Where a year earlier, Bethpage's greens appeared flat, here players had to detect deceptive slopes difficult to read because they blend so effectively into the landscape.

Dave Ward, the course superintendent, pointed at the sixth green, which at a quick glance seems flat.

"You have to look closely to see how the right-to-left slope is going with the topography. That fools a lot of people. All the greens have some of that."

Add those misleading slopes to Stimpmeter readings of 12 feet, and heartbeat rates rose to dangerous levels on every downhill putt. It explains why Mungeam rebuilt two greens: He had to create a few fairly level spots for a decent hole location.

Nevertheless, combine those slick, canted greens with deep bunkers, good length, fairways

17th PAR 3 247 YARDS

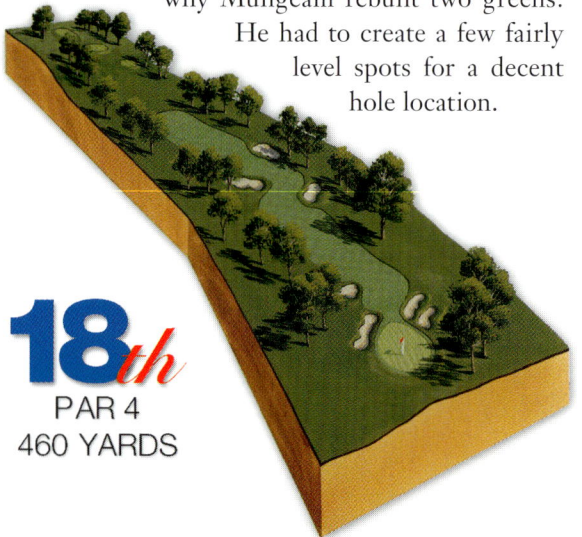

18th PAR 4 460 YARDS

squeezed to an average of 25 yards bordered by the usual U.S. Open rough and obviously the Open field had been asked to pass a severe test. Then too, perhaps the field had been asked as well to examine something special.

Over the last few decades, beginning with Pebble Beach in 1972, Shinnecock Hills in 1986, Pinehurst No. 2 in 1999 and Bethpage in 2002, the USGA had re-discovered a series of jewels. Now, as the events of June 2003 fade, we might reflect on how Olympia Fields held up against the world's premier golfers, who came equipped with all the best of modern technology, and ask if we have uncovered still another lost treasure.

The 18th hole, par 4 and 460 yards.

Bill Haas looks over his father's shoulder as Jay Haas makes a point to him and uncle Bob Goalby.

103rd U.S. OPEN Qualifying

For some years the United States Open Championship has ended on Father's Day, which adds a special glow to those times when fathers and sons have played together in this, the game's most important competition. In recent memory, Jack and Gary Nicklaus and Gary and Wayne Player played together, although in different years.

In times past, fathers and sons seemed traditional in the big golf events. The most famous of them all, of course, has to be Old Tom Morris and his son Tom Jr., who between them won eight British Open championships in the 1860s and 1870s. Willie Park and Willie Park Jr. won six together, four of those by the father. (Willie Jr. did the original design of the North Course at Olympia Fields.)

The 2003 championship was graced by Jay Haas and his son Bill, who had just completed his junior year at Wake Forest University. As a semi-finalist in the 2002 U.S. Amateur Championship, Bill Haas was exempt from local qualifying, and since Jay had tied for 12th place in the 2002 Open, he automatically had a place, exempt from all qualifying.

While having at least one father-son pair in the Open prompted a warm and fuzzy feeling, it didn't help the Haases' golf games. Off in the third group early Thursday morning, Bill shot 73 and beat his father by two strokes, but the next day Jay shot 72 and Bill had 76. Since the 36-hole cut fell at 143, neither survived until Father's Day.

Nor did Tom Glissmeyer.

The name Glissmeyer didn't strike fear into the hearts of veterans of golf's upper echelons in June 2003, but who knows the future? We do know, though, that young Tom, a slightly built young man with a pleasing manner, played in the Open, and he was just 16 years old, having completed the 10th grade at Cheyenne Mountain High School in Colorado Springs, Col. Young Tom succeeded while thousands of mature men failed. He survived two stages of qualifying and took his place among the elite 156 who made it to the Open.

Glissmeyer shot 80 and 79, and did not survive the 36-hole cut, which wasn't at all unusual. Winning a place is difficult in itself; scoring low enough to play the last two rounds asks for almost flawless golf. The ratio of entrants to qualifying places stacks the odds heavily against any player's getting that far.

When entries closed Wednesday, April 23, at 5 p.m., 7,820 had been accepted. Only 73 men escaped both qualifying rounds because, for example, they had won one of the last 10 Opens, the last five British Opens or PGA Championships, the last five Masters or the last U.S. Amateur and runner-up. More avoid qualifying through other playing records, but the rest faced the qualifying ordeal.

An additional 189 earned exemptions from local qualifying, which meant 7,558 entrants battled through local rounds for 540 places, and then, with the addition to the 189 otherwise exempt, 729 competed for just 83 places in sectional.

Some prominent players failed to qualify at all. A year earlier, Steve Elkington had tied Ernie Els, Thomas Levet and Stuart Appleby in a playoff for the British Open, and yet he didn't play well enough to win a place at Olympia Fields, even though he had been exempt from local qualifying.

Qualifying

Players Who Were Fully Exempt for the 2003 U.S. Open (73)

Robert Allenby 8, 9, 16	Jay Haas 8, 11, 16	Phil Mickelson 8, 9, 16
Stuart Appleby 16	Padraig Harrington 8, 10, 13, 16	Colin Montgomerie 10, 16
Ricky Barnes 2	Dudley Hart 8	Jose Maria Olazabal 3, 9, 10
Rich Beem 5, 9, 12, 16	Scott Hoch 8, 16	Mark O'Meara 4
Thomas Bjorn 10, 16	Charles Howell III 9, 16	Craig Parry 15, 16
Tom Byrum 8	Trevor Immelman 10, 16	Corey Pavin 1
Angel Cabrera 10, 16	Hale Irwin 17	Kenny Perry 9, 11, 12, 16
Michael Campbell 10, 16	Lee Janzen 1	Don Pooley 7
Paul Casey 16	Steve Jones (W) 1	Nick Price 8, 9, 16
K.J. Choi 9, 16	Jerry Kelly 9, 16	Chris Riley 9, 16
Darren Clarke 16	Tom Kite 17	Loren Roberts 9
Fred Couples 16	Bernhard Langer 16	John Rollins 9
Chris DiMarco 9, 16	Paul Lawrie 4, 10, 16	Eduardo Romero 10, 16
David Duval 4	Stephen Leaney 10	Justin Rose 10, 16
Ernie Els 1, 4, 9, 10, 11, 12, 13, 16	Justin Leonard 8, 9, 11, 16	Adam Scott 10, 16
	Peter Lonard 8, 15, 16	Vijay Singh 3, 5, 9, 11, 12, 16
Bob Estes 9, 16	Davis Love III 6, 9, 11, 12, 16	Jeff Sluman 9, 16
Nick Faldo 8	Steve Lowery 9	Toru Taniguchi 14
Niclas Fasth 16	Scott McCarron 9	David Toms 5, 9, 11, 16
Brad Faxon 16	Jeff Maggert 8	Kirk Triplett 16
Steve Flesch 16	Hunter Mahan 2	Scott Verplank 16
Fred Funk 9, 16	Shigeki Maruyama 9, 16	Tom Watson 17
Jim Furyk 9, 11, 16	Len Mattiace 9, 16	Mike Weir 3, 11, 12, 16
Sergio Garcia 8, 9, 10, 16	Billy Mayfair 8	Tiger Woods 1, 3, 4, 5, 8, 9, 11, 12, 16
Retief Goosen 1, 9, 10, 16	Rocco Mediate 9, 16	

Key to Player Exemptions:

1. Winners of the U.S. Open Championship for the last 10 years
2. Winner and runner-up of the 2002 U.S. Amateur Championship
3. Winners of the Masters Tournament the last five years
4. Winners of the British Open Championship the last five years
5. Winners of the PGA of America Championship the last five years
6. Winner of the 2003 Players Championship
7. Winner of the 2002 U.S. Senior Open Championship
8. From the 2002 U.S. Open Championship, the 15 lowest scorers and anyone tying for 15th place
9. From the 2002 final official PGA Tour money list, the top 30 money leaders
10. From the 2002 final official PGA European Tour, the top 15 money leaders
11. From the 2003 official PGA Tour money list, the top 10 money leaders through May 25
12. Any multiple winner of PGA Tour co–sponsored events whose victories are considered official from April 24, 2002 through June 1, 2003
13. From the 2003 PGA European Tour, the top two money leaders through May 26
14. From the 2002 final Japan Golf Tour money list, the top two leaders provided they are within the top 75 point leaders of the World Rankings at that time
15. From the 2002-2003 official PGA Tour of Australasia money list as of March 17, the top two leaders provided they are within the top 75 point leaders of the World Rankings at that time
16. From the World Rankings list, the top 50 point leaders as of May 26
17. Special exemptions selected by the USGA Executive Committee. International players not otherwise exempt as selected by the USGA Executive Committee

(W) Withdrew

Sectional Qualifying Results

Double Eagle Club and The Lakes Golf & Country Club
Columbus, Ohio
101 golfers for 20 qualifying spots
Stewart Cink, Duluth, Ga., 62-61–123
Tim Clark, South Africa, 64-68–132
Mark Calcavecchia, Phoenix, Ariz., 67-67–134
Brad Elder, Dallas, Texas, 67-67–134
Chris Smith, Peru, Ind., 67-68–135
Dean Wilson, Kaneohe, Hawaii, 67-69–136
Joe Ogilvie, Austin, Texas, 71-65–136
*John Bradley Holmes, Campbellsville, Ky., 69-67–136
Sean McCarty, Solon, Iowa, 70-66–136
Geoff Ogilvy, Australia, 70-66–136
Rory Sabbatini, Southlake, Texas, 68-68–136
Jonathan Kaye, Phoenix, Ariz., 70-66–136
Bob Tway, Edmond, Okla., 67-69–136
Tim Petrovic, Dade City, Fla., 70-67–137
Hiroshi Matsuo, Jupiter, Fla., 68-69–137
J.P. Hayes, El Paso, Texas, 67-70–137
Kevin Sutherland, Sacramento, Calif., 67-71–138
Jesper Parnevik, Sweden, 68-70–138
David Smail, New Zealand, 69-69–138
(P)Rob Bradley, Louisville, Ky., 70-69–139

Chad Campbell

Kirtland Country Club
Cleveland, Ohio
16 golfers for 1 qualifying spot
Chad Campbell, Lewisville, Texas, 72-67–139

Chevy Chase Club
Chevy Chase, Md.
38 players for 3 qualifying spots
Sean Murphy, Scottsdale, Ariz., 64-73–137
Dicky Pride, Orlando, Fla., 66-72–138
(P)Chris Anderson, Covina, Calif., 68-70–138

Stewart Cink

Rory Sabbatini

Jesper Parnevik

Qualifying

Woodmont Country Club
Rockville, Md.
156 players for 34 qualifying spots
*Bill Haas, Greer, S.C., 69-64–133
Rod Pampling, Australia, 64-69–133
Hidemichi Tanaka, Japan, 64-69–133
Marco Dawson, Lakeland, Fla., 66-68–134
Joe Durant, Molino, Fla., 64-70–134
Kent Jones, Albuquerque, N.M., 66-68–134
Joey Sindelar, Horseheads, N.Y., 66-68–134
Doug Labelle, Mt. Pleasant, Mich., 66-69–135
Jonathan Byrd, St. Simons Island, Ga., 69-67–136
Alex Cejka, Germany, 67-69–136
Brandt Jobe, Southlake, Texas, 67-69–136
Neal Lancaster, Smithfield, N.C., 68-68–136
Brett Quigley, Barrington, R.I., 71-65–136
Darron Stiles, Weaverville, N.C., 66-70–136
Mark Wurtz, La Quinta, Calif., 70-66–136
Craig Bowden, Bloomington, Ind., 68-69–137
Ryan Dillon, Aiken, S.C., 67-70–137
Dan Forsman, Provo, Utah, 67-70–137
Richard Johnson, Sweden, 64-73–137
Cliff Kresge, Apopka, Fla., 67-70–137
Spike McRoy, Huntsville, Ala., 68-69–137
Larry Mize, Columbus, Ga., 68-69–137
*Chez Reavie, Tempe, Ariz., 63-74–137
Tommy Armour, Dallas, Texas, 67-71–138
Woody Austin, Derby, Kan., 65-73–138
Jay Don Blake, Rockville, Mass., 70-68–138
Olin Browne, Jupiter, Fla., 65-73–138
Robert Damron, Orlando, Fla., 70-68–138
Brian Henninger, Wilsonville, Ore., 69-69–138
Roland Thatcher, The Woodlands, Texas, 65-73–138
Jay Williamson, St. Louis, Mo., 68-70–138
(P)Bob Burns, Valencia, Calif., 67-72–139
(P)Ian Leggatt, Canada, 66-73–139
(P)Brian Gay, Keene's Point, Fla., 71-68–139

Old Oaks Country Club and Century Country Club
Purchase, N.Y.
72 players for 4 qualifying spots
Fredrik Jacobson, Sweden, 68-70–138
Geoffrey Sisk, Marshfield, Mass., 73-67–140
John Maginnes, Greensboro, N.C., 72-68–140
(P)Cortney Brisson, Wallace, N.C., 72-70–142

Hidemichi Tanaka

Stonebridge Ranch
McKinney, Texas
35 golfers for 2 qualifying spots
*Trip Kuehne, Dallas, Texas, 62-73–135
(P)Greg Hiller, San Antonio, Texas, 69-68–137

Lake Nona Golf and Country Club
Orlando, Fla.
85 players for 5 qualifying spots
Maarten Lafeber, Holland, 69-70–139
Matt Seppanen, Orlando, Fla., 72-67–139
Alan Morin, Royal Palm Beach, Fla., 71-69–140
Grant Waite, New Zealand, 68-73–141
Doug Dunakey, Port Charlotte, Fla., 70-71–141

Larry Mize

Tom Glissmeyer

Bryce Molder

Columbine Country Club
Littleton, Colo.
29 golfers for 2 qualifying spots
Bret Guetz, Littleton, Colo., 67-69–136
*Tom Glissmeyer, Colorado Springs, Colo., 72-69–141

Ansley Golf Club's Settingown Creek
Roswell, Ga.
42 players for 2 qualifying spots
Luke List, Ringgold, Ga., 68-68–136
Billy Andrade, Atlanta, Ga., 68-69–137

El Caballero Country Club
Tarzana, Calif.
78 golfers for 4 qualifying spots
Bill Lunde, Las Vegas, Nev., 67-68–135
Anthony Arvidson, Scottsdale, Ariz., 71-67–138
*Rick Reinsberg, Lafayette, Calif., 69-69–138
Warren Schutte, Anthem, Ariz., 69-69–138

North Shore Country Club
Glenview, Ill.
61 golfers for 4 qualifying spots
Brian Davis, England, 68-66–134
Bryce Molder, Scottsdale, Ariz., 68-66–134
Tom Gillis, Lake Orion, Mich., 71-68–139
(P)Jason Knutzon, W. Des Moines, Iowa, 70-71–141

*Denotes amateur   (P) Won playoff

Washington National Golf Club
Auburn, Wash.
18 golfers for 1 qualifying spot
Chris Baryla, El Paso, Texas, 69-70–139

Milburne Golf Club
Kansas City, Mo.
23 golfers for 1 qualifying spot
Steve Gotsche, Great Bend, Kan., 70-69–139
Roy Biancalana, Mt. Prospect, Ill., 71-69–140 (alternate)

Robert Damron

Caddie Bruce Edwards and Tom Watson shared the stage, and Watson shot 65 to share the lead in the first round.

As the U.S. Open Championship approached, no one quite knew what to expect — and certainly not what happened.

On a cool, overcast day, 53-year-old Tom Watson holed a full-blooded 6-iron and eagled the 12th, birdied the seventh after a reluctant 45-foot putt hovered over the lip before it fell, and shot 65 while his caddie, Bruce Edwards, afflicted with an incurable disease, lugged his heavy bag. As well:

Brett Quigley, a 33-year-old journeyman who had made a career of qualifying tournaments, matched Watson's 65 with his father carrying his bag.

Even though someone had stolen his 2-iron, Brian Davis, an Englishman who had flown over to qualify 10 days earlier, played his first four holes in five under par before settling into his comfort zone and shooting 71.

Warming up for the first round, Ricky Barnes, the U.S. Amateur champion, swung so hard, the head of his driver flew off. He used what he could find — a club several inches shorter than his own — and often found himself in the rough, but still managed to shoot 71.

Tiger Woods, the defending champion, played a complete round with only one hole under par and finished the day at even-par 70.

Struck by back spasms on the 12th fairway, Hale Irwin, three times the U.S. Open champion, was taken from the course in a cart.

And the United States Golf Association, usually charged with intent to embarrass the game's leading players, found itself accused of making the golf course too easy. Go figure.

In truth, Olympia Fields Country Club, which is closer to Gary, Ind., than downtown Chicago, did pose a mystery. Except for a few Western Opens — the last 32 years earlier — it hadn't been tested in one of the game's four premier events since Jerry Barber bested Don January in the 1961 PGA Championship. And that had been 42 years ago, before Tom Watson had turned 12.

In support of the plaintiff, scores did seem unusually low. In addition to the 65s, Justin Leonard and Jay Don Blake shot 66, Jim Furyk and the Australian Stephen Leaney shot 67, three others shot 68, and 15 more came in with 69, among them Ernie Els, the British Open champion. That adds up to 24 men under par.

In defense of the USGA, Midwestern weather had not been ideal. Spring rains had softened the Olympia Fields greens to a point where early in the week they would hold almost any kind of shot, and cool temperatures had stunted the rough's growth and density. Even so, just 24 players of this caliber breaking par was not cause for panic. A day or so of sunshine fixed all that by the end.

Nevertheless, this had been a strange day, entirely normal for the Open.

Ranked as the second best player in the game, behind Woods, of course, Ernie Els played 17 holes in par and birdied only the 14th, while Blake, who had made only two 36-hole cuts all year, birdied five.

Colin Montgomerie birdied the difficult 12th, which allowed only 15 all day, yet bogeyed the sixth, which claimed just 16. He shot 69.

Meantime, with his usual enthusiastic gallery urging him on, Woods played a stunning iron shot into the sixth green and holed the putt for

First Round

Mike Weir (73) was set back by a three-hole stretch.

Davis Love III (76) was still mourning a death.

Padraig Harrington (69) finished with a bogey.

an eagle 3, the highlight of his day. One under par then, he struggled to hold on but lost a stroke at the ninth, his 18th of the day. He drove into the right rough, pulled his approach into the left greenside bunker, played a loose recovery and bogeyed to finish at even par.

Meantime, others had problems. Mike Weir, the toast of Canada after winning the Masters two months earlier, played the eighth, ninth, and 10th in 17 strokes against a par of 12, and, with the help of two birdies, shot 73, three over par, buried in a tie for 81st place. Davis Love III had worse problems.

Looking early in the year as if he might win anything, Love had been shaken recently by the suicide of his brother-in-law, the husband of his wife's sister. With total faith in Jeff Knight, Davis had given him control of some of his finances and the responsibility for running his household. Lately Knight had been suspected of stealing from the accounts. When the allegations surfaced, Knight shot himself.

Love hadn't been the same since. He had won three tournaments in the early months, but here he played poor golf, bogeyed six holes and double-

First Round

Tom Watson	65	-5
Brett Quigley	65	-5
Justin Leonard	66	-4
Jay Don Blake	66	-4
Stephen Leaney	67	-3
Jim Furyk	67	-3
Tom Gillis	68	-2
Mark Calcavecchia	68	-2
Ian Leggatt	68	-2

The feature group consisted of U.S. Amateur champion Ricky Barnes (left), Ernie Els and Tiger Woods.

bogeyed another. He birdied only the sixth, which he reached in two shots, and the 12th. Out in 40, he came back in 36 and shot 76, leaving little hope he would survive for the weekend.

Then there was Phil Mickelson, runner-up to Woods a year earlier. Mickelson began by dumping his drive into a fairway bunker and dropping a stroke at the 10th, but he fought back well enough to finish on even par, lots better than David Duval.

Poor Duval. Once a major force in the game, a man who shot 59 at the 1999 Bob Hope tournament, Duval had sunk into a severe slump. Starting from the 10th tee, he played his first five holes in five over par, shot 40 on the second nine, then 38 on the first nine, even though he birdied both the fourth, a par 3, and the weak sixth. He turned in a 78. The second round would be a formality. He was finished.

With the starting field split so that half started at the first tee and half at the 10th, half in the morning and half in the afternoon, the group of Woods, Els and Barnes played the early shift; both Watson and Quigley played in the afternoon. By then they had their target scores.

Both Leonard and Blake drew morning times as well, and they, not Woods and Els, set the standard.

Leonard teed off in mid-morning, 40 minutes ahead of Blake, grouped with the Irishman Padraig Harrington, a threat in any competition, and Charles Howell III, a slender wisp just a week short of his 24th birthday. Harrington finished among

Phil Mickelson (70) overcame three bogeys.

First Round

Justin Leonard (66) had nine one-putt greens.

the 15 at 69, and Howell matched Woods and 18 others at 70.

When he won the 1997 British Open, Leonard had made up five strokes with a blistering last round of 67 over the brutal Royal Troon course, and now he played his lowest U.S. Open round. Starting from the first tee, he birdied both the second and third holes, and when he rolled in a 10-foot putt at the ninth, the first birdie of the day there, he made the turn in 34, two under par.

It had been quite a trip. Playing scattershot golf, Leonard had hit only three of the seven fairways on driving holes and six greens, but relying on his deadly putting stroke, he bogeyed only the fifth, the toughest par on the course. His par 5 at the sixth probably meant he gave half a stroke to the field.

With his driver settling down on the homeward nine, Leonard hit every fairway, missed only two greens, and came back in 32, a bogey 5 at the 12th his only blemish.

Blake had led the Open once before. He had shot 66 in the opening round at Oak Hill in 1989, but he never approached it again that week and finished in a tie for 18th place. Here he played steady, although not spectacular, tee-to-green golf, and putted quite well. Of his eight one-putt greens, he

Stephen Leaney (67) birdied both par 3s at the end.

Jim Furyk (67) needed to rally from two over par.

Jay Don Blake (66) had eight one-putt greens.

Chad Campbell (70) had the 7 a.m. honor on the first tee.

holed five for birdies and saved his pars at the testing fifth, 12th and 17th, the long par 3.

After birdieing the second, he holed from about six feet at the sixth to go two under par, then ran in another at the eighth. When the putt dropped, Blake was three under and held a share of the lead at that point of the day with Montgomerie and Tom Gillis, a 34-year-old American refugee from the European, African and Asian tours.

In the first group off the 10th tee, Gillis stepped onto the 17th tee one over par. There his fortunes changed. He birdied, added another at the 18th, moved over to the first tee and birdied once more, and then scored a fourth consecutive birdie at the second. Since he had teed off before either Blake or Montgomerie, Gillis had the clear lead.

Quickly he dropped a stroke at the third, won it back at the sixth, but lost it again by bogeying the hard ninth, which stretched 496 yards. With 68, he positively glowed. Through his extensive travels, he had often asked himself what he was doing with

Hidemichi Tanaka (69) led off from the 10th tee.

First Round

Brett Quigley (65) ran off six consecutive 3s.

Mark Calcavecchia (68) birdied the 18th.

Ian Leggatt (68) posted three birdies, one bogey.

his life. For a short time he thought he knew.

Delayed by heavy rains that held the finish of the PGA Tour event near Washington, D.C., over until Monday, Quigley arrived at Olympia Fields in time for only two practice rounds. Hardly enough, one would think, for someone who had missed the cut in his two previous Opens. Instead, Quigley believed it improved his focus.

Perhaps he was right. Or else Brian Davis inspired him. Grouped together, Quigley watched as Davis dipped five under after four holes, then realized that after birdieing the sixth, he stood three under par himself.

Then Quigley ran into trouble at the seventh, a 212-yard par 3 played from an elevated tee to a green bordered by Butterfield Creek. His ball missed the green and sank into the water. His father, who was also his caddie, advised him to take the penalty stroke and drop out, but Quigley voted against it.

"This is the U.S. Open," he insisted. "I've got to go in and get it."

Taking his wedge, Quigley hit his ball on the green but left himself a lengthy putt and bogeyed.

Out in 34, Quigley dropped another stroke at the 10th, which was not a difficult hole, but in quick order he slipped back into an attacking mode and birdied the 12th, 13th and 14th, parred the 15th and birdied the 16th. When he parred the 17th he had run off six consecutive 3s. He came back in 31 for his 65, the clear leader, since he had finished well ahead of Watson.

No matter all that had gone on — Quigley's theatrics, Davis's amazing start — this day belonged to Watson and to Edwards.

By June of 2003, Watson approached his 54th birthday. Because he had built such a marvelous career record — 1982 Open champion, winner of two Masters Tournaments along with five British Opens — the USGA had extended him a special exemption into the championship. He repaid the favor by thrilling the galleries.

With temperatures hovering in the high 50s and the sun blocked by threatening gray cloud cover, and with his long-time caddie at his side, Watson raced around Olympia Fields in the lowest score he had shot in the Open since his 65 in the 1987 championship at The Olympic Club in San Francisco. Scott Simpson had beaten him by one stroke that week by playing the last five holes in three under par. It had been Watson's last best chance to add another of the game's premier championships to his record.

For a time the most dangerous player in the game, aside from Jack Nicklaus, Watson had lost this standing long ago. But here, for one brief afternoon, it had returned.

After an opening bogey at the 10th hole, Watson began to feel it at the 12th, his third hole of the round. His drive sitting in the fairway, deep in the valley between tee and green, Watson asked Edwards the yardage to the green, set high above.

It was a day that everyone would remember.

Edwards told him 178 yards. Watson pulled out his 6-iron and ripped another of his old precise shots dead at the flagstick.

Neither man could see the ball come down, but when the gallery roared, they knew it had dived into the hole for an eagle 2. Watson was on his way.

Another birdie at the 16th and he played the second nine in 32. Three more on the first nine and Watson had caught Quigley, a more than satisfying day for one who played most of his golf against seniors.

While it had been Watson's name that went up on the leaderboard, Tom had played only one part in the drama at Olympia Fields. Bruce Edwards had shared the stage.

Edwards had begun carrying Watson's bag 30 years earlier, and had stuck with him except for a three-year period when, at Watson's suggestion, he had switched to Greg Norman. He went back to Watson when Norman's game turned sour.

Edwards had reached the age of 48 by 2003, and had married early in the year. When he complained of trouble manipulating his fingers, Watson insisted he consult a doctor. He was diagnosed with amyotrophic lateral sclerosis — Lou Gehrig's disease — which is steadily degenerative and always fatal. There is no cure.

Understanding Edwards's physical limits, the USGA offered him a cart, but he turned it down; he would walk the course as he had always done, out there beside Watson.

The fans felt for him and cheered for them both on every hole.

As they walked off the last green together, tears welling in both their eyes, the gallery rose and applauded until, an inseparable pair, they disappeared into the scorer's shack.

103rd U.S. OPEN
Second Round

After a day of nostalgia, watching Tom Watson relive his glory years, fans saw more high drama as Vijay Singh matched the U.S. Open's 18-hole record by burning the grass off Olympia Fields with a round of 63, and Tiger Woods showed signs of renewed life by shooting 66 and thrusting himself back into the Open.

Neither round affected the championship so much as Jim Furyk's 66, which shot him to the top of the standing alongside Singh, and, by the way, broke the existing 36-hole record of 134 Jack Nicklaus had set at Baltusrol 23 years earlier. The 134 had been equaled by Chen Tze-Chung (T.C. Chen) at Oakland Hills in 1985, Lee Janzen at Baltusrol in 1993 and Woods at Pebble Beach in 2000.

Furyk and Singh led the Open with 133, two strokes ahead of 25-year-old Jonathan Byrd and Stephen Leaney, who shared third place at 135. Byrd shot 69-66 and Leaney 67-68.

Watson slipped from an opening 65 to 72 and dropped from a tie for first to a share of 10th place, at 137, while Brett Quigley dropped from first to a tie for 18th, following his opening 65 with 74.

Woods, meantime, climbed from a share of 25th place to a tie for fifth along with Justin Leonard, Nick Price, Eduardo Romero and Fredrik Jacobson. Woods got there with some of his usual dramatics, playing one shot through an impossibly narrow gap in the trees off the first fairway that set up one birdie, then a sweeping slice around more trees off the sixth for another. The shots drove the gallery wild, and set other players' pulses racing.

Par took another pounding. Once a standard of excellence, at Olympia Fields par became little more than a convenient means of keeping score. After 36 holes, the Open field had played 62 rounds in the 60s, 38 of them in the second round. Only Baltusrol had given up more, yielding 76 in 1993. Even Merion had yielded only 58, and that wonderful old course had measured less than 6,600 yards in 1981, the shortest Open course since the end of the Second World War.

Even Singh's record-matching 63 beat the day's next best score by one bare stroke. Woody Austin, who hardly anyone knew had made the field, shot 64, one better than Price's 65, and Woods, Furyk, Byrd, Romero and the Czech Alex Cejka shot 66.

Par as the measure of first-class golf had been a longstanding creed within the United States Golf Association. To back up its position, officials felt they need look for proof no further than at winning scores in previous Opens. As late as 2002 even par took second place at Bethpage State Park, on Long Island, N.Y. Only Tiger Woods, the champion, bested regulation figures by playing four rounds in 277 strokes, three under standard figures, over a brutish course where the field's average 18-hole score was nearly 75 strokes.

Before taking the U.S. Open to Chicago, the USGA asked for comprehensive renovation to assure a course that hadn't seen an Open in 75 years — the days of Bob Jones and Walter Hagen — could cope with 21st century golfers.

After two rounds under attack by current golfers with modern clubs and golf balls, reports that the remodeling had worked seemed exaggerated. Instead of challenging the game's best players, the USGA appeared to coddle them.

As evidence, one record broken that had stood

Vijay Singh (133) missed the green at the 18th and finished with par and 63 to tie the single-round record.

Second Round

Woody Austin (138) shot 64 with seven birdies.

Tom Watson (137) double-bogeyed the 12th.

Second Round

Vijay Singh	70 - 63	– 133	-7
Jim Furyk	67 - 66	– 133	-7
Jonathan Byrd	69 - 66	– 135	-5
Stephen Leaney	67 - 68	– 135	-5
Justin Leonard	66 - 70	– 136	-4
Fredrik Jacobson	69 - 67	– 136	-4
Tiger Woods	70 - 66	– 136	-4
Eduardo Romero	70 - 66	– 136	-4
Nick Price	71 - 65	– 136	-4
Tom Watson	65 - 72	– 137	-3
Robert Damron	69 - 68	– 137	-3

for nearly a quarter of a century and another tied that had lasted 30 years. Back in 1973, Johnny Miller stunned proud old Oakmont Country Club with his astonishing final-round 63 and snatched the championship. Nicklaus and Tom Weiskopf matched the 63 in the first round at Baltusrol in 1980. It hadn't been touched since.

Second-round scores worked wonders in 2003. Singh climbed from a tie for 25th into a tie for first, Austin jumped 80 places into a tie for 12th, and Price moved 40 places into a tie for fifth.

Even the players agreed the Olympia Fields setup seemed fair, their code word for easy. Still, the USGA hierarchy held firm to its conviction that Olympia Fields would strike back if only the clouds would roll by and the wind sweep in.

Of course, a fair number saw no need to toughen Olympia Fields any further. It played hard enough as is.

Both Watson and Quigley had faded into the crowd. Brian Davis, five under after his first four holes on Thursday, played his next 32 in eight over par, and with 143, barely survived into the weekend.

Then we had Jay Don Blake, four under par in the first round with 66, and seven over in the second at 77. From one off the lead, he barely made the cut and fell 10 strokes behind, at 143. Nevertheless, he did better than Tom Gillis. The clear leader at three under par after 11 holes on Thursday, and only three behind at the end of the day, Gillis followed his opening 68 with 76 and missed the cut.

By the time Singh started out, just before 1 p.m., Furyk had finished and put his 133 on the board. It gave Singh something to aim for, and he went after it from the start. Driving better than he had in the first round, when he hit only five fairways all day, Singh ripped one down the middle at the first hole. Then, short of the green with his 3-wood, his ball resting about 30 feet from the hole, Singh chipped in for an eagle 3 and moved two under. On to the second, a 400-yard par 4 whose fairway swings left beyond the drive zone. He hit another solid drive, then a 9-iron to 10 feet. The putt dropped for a birdie 3 and he went three under after two holes.

A stroke lost at the third, a loosely played hole, where from a decent position following a 6-iron tee shot, Singh dumped his pitch into the right greenside bunker. He flew his recovery over the green, pitched to about two feet and holed for a bogey 5. Back to two under.

Another nicely played 8-iron to about 10 feet and Singh scored 2 at the fourth. Three under again with the wimpish sixth hole coming up.

Safely past the dangerous fifth, Singh missed

Stephen Leaney (135) shot 68 with two birdies.

Phil Mickelson (140), who had two 70s, rejoiced when his birdie putt fell on the 17th.

Second Round

Justin Leonard (136) had four bogeys, four birdies.

Jonathan Byrd (135) eagled the first (his 10th).

his first fairway at the sixth, leaving himself little chance of hitting the green, which he should reach routinely after a well-placed drive. Instead, he laid up with a 6-iron, pitched on to about 15 feet, then three-putted. Another wasted stroke, back to two under.

A routine par 3 at the deceptive seventh, and then Singh had his second straight missed fairway at the eighth. No great problem. He hit the green, took two putts, then moved onto the long ninth still two under par. Another par 4 there, and with 34, he had played the first nine as well as he had played it in the first round.

There the similarity ended. Starting from the 10th tee on Thursday, Singh had shot 36, two over par. On this day he battered the second nine by shooting 29, only the third 29 ever shot in the Open. Curiously, Neal Lancaster had shot both, the first at Shinnecock Hills back in 1995 and the second at Oakland Hills the following year. It helped him to shoot 65 and tie for fourth in 1995, but he finished far back in 1996.

Singh hit every green but the last on the homeward nine, missed just two fairways and holed some sizable putts — from 30 feet at the 10th, 18 feet at the 11th and a bit over 20 feet at the 15th, another par 3 played from a high tee.

Singh also lofted a sand wedge to about 10 feet at the 13th and holed it, then played a lovely 8-iron inside six feet and birdied the 14th.

It was there that a rowdy spectator taunted Singh about Annika Sorenstam, the woman golfer who had played in a PGA Tour event at Colonial Country Club, in Fort Worth, Texas, a few weeks earlier. Singh had been candid in opposing her playing, and he had been criticized ever since.

When Singh missed holing his pitch, the spectator suggested Annika would have made it. Further words were spoken, and the spectator found himself watching the Open from somewhere other than Olympia Fields.

Unperturbed, Singh holed the putt.

Now he stood seven under par with three holes to play. With luck he could shoot 62, a new low, or perhaps 61.

He nearly pulled it off. He missed from 12 feet at the 16th, and his birdie putt from eight feet at the 17th caught the edge of the hole but swerved away. Short of the 18th with his second, Singh putted from about three feet off the green, but his ball broke away and he made his third straight par. Back in 29, he had his 63.

Later Singh admitted he had three-putted the sixth through carelessness. Play had been slow, and he had waited for some time before playing his second shot.

Because of the delay, Singh claimed, "I hit my first putt in a hurry, and I didn't want to wait any longer, so I went on and finished. It was my mistake. I should have taken a bit more time and played at my pace. But things happen."

In the end, he had caught Furyk.

Among the early starters from the first tee, grouped with Phil Mickelson and husky, good-natured Irishman Darren Clarke, Furyk played a nearly errorless and rare bogey-free round. He had played the first nine in 31 strokes the previous day, but here he shot 34, two under par, birdieing the first and sixth, the two par-5 holes. With his drive in the rough off the first fairway, he played a 3-wood second just short of the green, pitched inside three feet and holed the putt. Routine pars followed at the next three holes, then another birdie at the sixth. On the green with a 4-wood second, Furyk got down in two from 40 feet, then parred the rest of the outward nine holes.

While he had played precision golf, his first nine did look dull. He had hit every green and two-putted all but the first, where he had holed a putt no one should miss.

The second nine didn't quite mirror the first, but it was close. He hit all but one fairway and missed just the 11th green. No matter, a nice chip saved another par.

Still two under, Furyk picked up two more birdies, playing a wedge to 10 feet at the 13th and an 8-iron even closer at the 14th. And these were not the club's easiest holes.

All two-putt pars the rest of the way, and Furyk had set a new Open record. Only Singh caught him.

For a time, though, Woods looked as if he might take command, playing his familiar swashbuckling game, laced with impossible shots and

Jim Furyk (133) shot 66, hitting 17 greens in regulation.

Second Round

David Toms (139) recovered from an opening 72.

Eduardo Romero (136) made eagle-3 on the first hole.

Nick Price (136) shot 65 with one bogey.

Fredrik Jacobson (136) had scores of 69 and 67.

eagle-eyed putting. Erratic drives had haunted him through the first round. Off among the early afternoon starters, Woods played more loose drives on the opening holes.

It seems strange somehow that certain players tend to play their bad shots consistently either right or left. Jack Nicklaus usually hit his bad shots left. Tiger Woods, on the other hand, leans toward hitting them right — not always but usually. He had shown it most noticeably at Royal Lytham and St. Annes during the 2001 British Open. From the seventh tee in the third round, he flew his drive so far into a heavy stand of trees he had to declare it unplayable. He'd had to put another ball in play back at the tee and take the penalty.

Now he did it again on the first hole, pushing his drive over the gallery ropes, over the gallery itself and in among another stand of trees. Luckily here, his ball settled on a relatively clean lie with the green visible through a narrow gap in the trees. Ever the magician, Woods drilled his ball right through the gap into a greenside bunker, popped the ball out and holed from 15 feet. He had made a birdie where anything might have been possible.

Tiger Woods (136) was erratic off the tees, but still shot 66 with six birdies.

Still playing like Merlin, he holed another putt from at least 50 feet and birdied the fourth, but quickly gave it back by taking a bogey 5 at the hard fifth, where his approach pulled up short of the green.

Now he played another of those improbable shots. The sixth fairway swings decidedly to the right, the direct line to the green blocked by more forestry. Once again Woods lost his drive to the right, but from a lie in the rough and his ball in such a position he couldn't see the green, he played a wide, sweeping slice that shot off toward trouble on the left, made a sharp right-hand turn, carried onto the green and died no more than 15 feet from the hole. With two putts he had another birdie.

By then Woods had run out of miracles, but, truly, he didn't need them. A straightforward birdie at the ninth and he went out in 33. Coming back he dropped a shot at the 11th, where he missed the green, birdied both the 13th and 16th through precise irons inside 10 feet, and came back in 33 as well. With 66, he had done what he had planned to: He had put himself in position to win.

Others, of course, had not. The 36-hole cut fell at 143, the lowest it had even fallen for a U.S. Open. It eliminated 88 men, a group that included Corey Pavin and Tom Kite, two former Open champions.

There were others as well. Rich Beem, the 2002 PGA champion, had played badly, and with 150 missed the cut by seven strokes. Even though he had won three tournaments and led the PGA Tour's money list, Davis Love III played one stroke worse than Beem and missed as well.

Both Jay Haas and his son, Bill, also missed the cut, Jay at 147 and Bill at 149.

Then there was young Tom Glissmeyer. Glissmeyer opened with 80 and pledged to himself he would not shoot that high a score again. He didn't. He played the second round in 79, hung around the rest of the week and spent lots of time on the practice tee, right next to Tiger Woods.

With the clock tower in the background, Jim Furyk (200) played to the 10th while setting the 54-hole scoring record.

103rd U.S. OPEN Third Round

Not content with breaking the U.S. Open's 36-hole scoring record, Jim Furyk lowered the 54-hole record by three strokes as well. Along the way he joined Gil Morgan and Tiger Woods in dipping 10 under par by birdieing the sixth hole of the third round. He had begun the third round at seven under par, then birdied the fourth, fifth and sixth. Only those three have gone as low as 10 under during an Open — not Hogan, not Nicklaus, not Palmer.

Furyk shot 67, his third consecutive round in the 60s, and not only set the record, he took control of the championship too. At the end of the day he found Stephen Leaney closest to him. A fairly obscure Australian who had gone through five PGA Tour qualifying tournaments without succeeding, Leaney lagged three strokes behind at 203, which, by the way, matched the former record. George Burns had shot 203 at Merion in 1981, then Chen Tze-Chung (T.C. Chen) matched it at Oakland Hills in 1985, and then Lee Janzen, at Baltusrol in 1993.

For a time early in the afternoon, Nick Price had shot to the front with a flurry of birdies, but his game cooled, and after a series of bogeys, he finished with 69 and slipped back to third place at 205, alongside Vijay Singh, who followed his 63 of Friday with 72 on Saturday.

Meantime, instead of the kind of roar that figured to strike fear into the hearts of anyone ahead of him, Tiger Woods played like a kitten and put up his worst score in an Open since be became a professional late in 1996. He shot 75, which wasn't all that bad. But everything is relative.

At 211 for 54 holes, Woods had fallen 11 strokes behind Furyk, wallowing in 24th place with eight others. Still, with him around, anything was possible, though unlikely.

While Price and Singh foundered, others moved up. Dicky Pride shot 66, the best round of the day, and climbed from the depths of a tie for 27th place into a fifth-place tie at 206 with Jonathan Byrd, Eduardo Romero and Ian Leggatt, a Canadian who shot his second 68.

Billy Mayfair, Mark O'Meara and Mark Calcavecchia shot 67s and climbed into a tie for ninth at 207. Mike Weir showed signs of life by shooting 67 and 68 in his last two rounds, although at 208 he had lots of ground to make up. Ernie Els and Justin Leonard were tied for 12th with Weir.

The sun burned down on Olympia Fields for a change, raising the temperature and soaking up moisture. With the greens firming up, scores in general climbed higher. Of the 68 men who survived the 36-hole cut, 15 scored in the 60s, quite a drop from the 38 who broke par in the third round.

Pride's showing had been the least expected of all. To win a place in the field, he had gone through both local and sectional qualifying, then hung around by shooting 71 and 69 in the first two rounds. Actually, he was lucky to have been playing at all. A year and a half earlier he had nearly died following gall bladder surgery. Now he stared in wonder at how well he had played.

"I can't really explain it," he said, "but everything has been clicking this week."

Not clicking as well as Furyk, even though Furyk's bogey-free stretch ran out at the 10th, where he missed both fairway and green and two-

Third Round

Nick Price (205) birdied five of the first six holes.

Third Round

Jim Furyk	67 - 66 - 67 – 200	-10
Stephen Leaney	67 - 68 - 68 – 203	-7
Nick Price	71 - 65 - 69 – 205	-5
Vijay Singh	70 - 63 - 72 – 205	-5
Dicky Pride	71 - 69 - 66 – 206	-4
Ian Leggatt	68 - 70 - 68 – 206	-4
Eduardo Romero	70 - 66 - 70 – 206	-4
Jonathan Byrd	69 - 66 - 71 – 206	-4
Mark O'Meara	72 - 68 - 67 – 207	-3
Mark Calcavecchia	68 - 72 - 67 – 207	-3
Billy Mayfair	69 - 71 - 67 – 207	-3

putted for a 5, one over par.

By then Furyk had fallen behind Price, four groups ahead of him. One of the game's finest ball-strikers and all-around good guys, Price began the round at four under par. By the time he had finished the sixth hole, he stood nine under, two ahead of Furyk, who had yet to make his first birdie, and one ahead of Singh.

Price had jumped ahead by birdieing five of the first six holes, one of the hottest streaks of his career. He began this scoring frenzy at the first, holing a birdie putt from perhaps 20 feet, added another at the second with a 3-wood and pitching wedge to eight feet, birdied the third by playing his tee shot with a 5-iron to stay short of Butterfield Creek, which knifes across the fairway, then a precise 145-yard 9-iron to maybe 10 feet. Still another putt dropped at the fourth, at 164 yards the shortest hole on the course. Here Price played an 8-iron and holed from six feet, ending a burst that had moved him ahead of both Furyk and Singh, who had barely begun.

After a struggling par 4 at the fifth, where he missed both the fairway and green, Price hit a drive and 5-iron to about 25 feet at the sixth. Two putts gave him still another birdie to go nine under par.

The fun ended there. Price played what he called "a really good 5-iron" from the seventh tee, but said later he had picked the wrong club. His ball plugged in the upslope of the left greenside bunker,

Dicky Pride (206) held on for 66 after making four birdies on the first nine.

and he said he did well to bogey. One stroke was gone. Another dropped at the ninth, where he misjudged the break of a big, sweeping 35-footer and three-putted.

Out in 33, Price had lost his touch by then. He started back with bogeys on both the 11th and 12th, a run of lost strokes on three of four holes, and came back in 36, two over par for the home nine, and shot 69. At five under par, he still lay behind Furyk and Singh, and had been passed by Leaney, who had been paired with Byrd in the next-to-last group.

It could have been worse. Nine feet from the hole after two shots at the 17th, a par 3, Price holed the putt, then laid an 8-iron within holing distance and birdied the 18th.

It had been a disappointing finish, especially after that blazing start. Looking back on it, Price said, "Oh, man, you dream about starting like that in a major championship," then added, "It was a lot of fun."

Mark O'Meara (207) shot 67 to move into the top 10.

Third Round

Tiger Woods (211) took a bogey 5 here on the fifth hole, and had a 75 with five bogeys.

Kenny Perry (212) came back with 69.

Which is more than Woods could say. He had been playing directly behind Price and found he could do very little right. He missed fairways, missed greens, and when he did hit a green, his ball usually settled miles from the hole. And then there was the whistle.

With his drive safely in the first fairway, Woods drew back his 3-wood for the second shot. Part way through the downswing, too late to stop, someone whistled — a shrill, piercing sound that couldn't be ignored. Appreciating neither the whistle nor the shot, Woods dropped his club, spouted a curse and glared toward the gallery. No one confessed, nor could anyone be sure if the whistler had intended to upset Woods or call his dog.

Nevertheless, it had put Woods in a sour mood, which didn't help his golf game. He scored four 5s on the first nine, only two for pars, went out in 38, bogeyed four more on the second nine,

Eduardo Romero (206) posted his second 70.

birdied only the 14th, came back in 37, three over par, and wrote 75 on his scorecard.

To the end he insisted he did not play badly.

"I hit a lot of good shots," Woods claimed, "but made nothing. When you're not making any putts, you can't get any momentum going."

Actually, he had played some loose golf and seldom put himself in position to hole a reasonable putt. He hit nine fairways and 12 greens, which is survivable with sharp close work around the greens, but on this day the tiger meowed.

Singh, of course, played nothing like he had a day earlier, although he opened with 34, the same as when he had shot 63. His second nine was another matter. Where he had shot 29 in the second round, here he had a terrible closing nine, shot nine strokes worse, with 38, and bogeyed the last three holes.

Clearly upset over his finish, Singh couldn't

Vijay Singh (205) bogeyed the last three holes.

Third Round

Ernie Els (208) shot 69 with four birdies.

Ian Leggatt (206) eagled the sixth, then bogeyed twice.

Jonathan Byrd (206) was enjoying the challenge.

understand why he lost so many strokes.

"There's no reason to finish with those three bogeys," Singh said. "I played okay. I just hit a couple of bad shots and had a bad lie on 18," where he missed the fairway and misdirected his approach into a grandstand. Given a penalty-free drop from an obstruction, Singh pitched on and two-putted. He shot 72, no longer one of the leaders.

Possibly more than most, Leaney appreciated his position, within three strokes of first place. "I've never been here before," he marveled, "and I'm not going to kid myself."

Leaney began by birdieing the first hole after a drive and then a 3-iron just short of the green, and a little shot to three feet. He made his next birdie at the fifth, among the more dangerous holes on any course. He played a fine drive and followed with a 6-iron and a good putt for another birdie.

Mark Calcavecchia (207) birdied three of the first four.

Two under par for the day and seven under for the distance, Leaney couldn't shake Furyk. He had matched Leaney's birdie at the fifth and moved further ahead by adding another at the sixth, where he recovered nicely from a greenside bunker.

After three routine pars, Leaney ripped a drive so far up the ninth fairway it left him nothing more than a 9-iron. The ball braked about five feet above the hole, leaving him a nervous downhill putt. Trying for nothing more than a safe two-putt, Leaney holed it. Out in 33, he was three under for the day, eight under for 45 holes.

There the party ended. He butchered the 10th and double-bogeyed, then three-putted the 11th, wiping out all the strokes he had won through the first nine holes. Birdies at the 15th and 18th, where he played a stunning 7-iron to about two feet, won back two strokes, and with 68, Leaney had played

Stephen Leaney (203) dropped three on the 10th and 11th.

Third Round

Billy Mayfair (207) had 67, his second in the 60s.

Mike Weir (208) was out in 32 with an eagle at No. 6.

Justin Leonard (208) tied for 12th after his 72.

all three rounds in the 60s.

But then, so had Furyk, and his added up to a lower number. So far Furyk had shot two 67s and a 66 and found himself treading ground no one had explored. He had done it with steady consistency. Through three rounds over an Open course that, truthfully, had not punished mis-played shots as severely as the USGA had planned, Furyk had played 54 holes with a scant six bogeys, half of them on the second nine of the first round, and two more on the home nine of the third round.

He had also scored 16 birdies — six on the first nine of the opening round. He had made five more birdies in the third round, going out in 33 and coming in with 34 for his 67. At the end of the day he stood 10 under par, three strokes clear of the field, a nice position for the final day.

Except for missing the first fairway, he played solid tee-to-green golf through the early holes but left himself little chance for birdies. He picked up

Jim Furyk (200) had played 54 holes with six bogeys.

his first birdie at the fifth, which gave up only 10 all day. Driving into prime position, he played a lovely 7-iron about four feet from the hole and coaxed it in for the 3.

It had been a satisfying hole, one that Furyk believed had a calming effect. He certainly played solid golf through the rest of the day.

One under, he birdied the sixth as well, recovering smartly from a greenside bunker and holing from less than a yard. At the ninth, a hole with what seemed an unreasonable combination of 496 yards and a par of 4, Furyk played his second shot with a wedge to within six feet and ran it in for his third birdie. Length has become irrelevant.

Out in 33, he played the home nine in 34, even par, with a bit of nail-biting at the end.

Playing a 3-iron from the 17th tee, Furyk put more into the shot than he should have and flew his ball to the back of the green. Left with a very long putt, he coaxed it within about six feet of the hole, then mis-played the second.

"I don't know how you leave one of those short," he said, "but I managed to do it."

A bogey 4 on a 247-yard par 3, and Furyk went on to the 18th.

With the wind behind him, Furyk felt he could carry a fairway bunker along the right, but he pulled the drive slightly. It missed the right bunker, then jumped over another guarding the left. From there he played a wedge to about 25 feet.

A par would give him 68 and a 54-hole score of 201, still under the record, but after studying the lie, Furyk stepped up to the ball and rammed it home.

New ground.

Jim Furyk (272) was challenged primarily by Stephen Leaney, and Furyk's 72 was good for a three-stroke victory.

103rd U.S. OPEN
Fourth Round

Over the last two days, Jim Furyk had broken one U.S. Open record and tied another, and now, going into the final round, he seemed certain to break a third. Jack Nicklaus had lowered the 72-hole record to 272 strokes in 1980, Lee Janzen matched it in 1993, and Tiger Woods followed in 2000.

Leading by three strokes as the 2003 championship drew to its close with a record 54-hole score of 200, Furyk seemed certain to set still another record, since he hadn't yet shot higher than 68.

At day's end, he shot 72 and simply matched the record. But he did win the championship, the climax of his 10-year career. His loopy, unorthodox swing had held up where other, more classic, styles had failed.

Stephen Leaney shot 72 as well and finished where he had started — in second place, three strokes behind, with 275.

Both Nick Price and Vijay Singh, who had been expected to put pressure on Furyk, played badly and moved backward. Tiger Woods, who improved only slightly over his third-round 75, shot 72 and, like Leaney, finished the day where he had started — 11 strokes back at 283.

Price fell into a tie for fifth by shooting 75 and 280, and Singh played worse, shot 78 and dropped into a tie for 20th alongside Woods.

Kenny Perry had come into the Open as the hottest player in the game, the winner at Colonial and the Memorial leading up to the Open, but he had been silent through the first three rounds. Sunday he shot 67, the best round of the day, and jumped 30 places into third place, tied with Mike Weir, the Masters winner.

Crowds began pouring onto the grounds early in the day, many of them to get a glimpse of Woods, who teed off just after noon, and to give themselves time to pass through security checks, where fans backed up in lines to have their bags rummaged through in the hunt for weapons and their bodies patted down.

They were brought to this suburb 25 miles south of Chicago by trains that stopped just outside the club's gates, by cars and by busses, then ferried from remote parking lots by fleets of school busses.

Those who arrived earliest could watch players with familiar names. Retief Goosen, the 2001 Open champion, teed off at 10:30, just behind Brian Davis, the Englishman who had led briefly early in the first round.

Phil Mickelson, second to Woods a year ago but nowhere near the leaders this week, followed Goosen, and Fred Couples, Sergio Garcia, Colin Montgomerie, Bernhard Langer and Padraig Harrington were in later groups. Tom Watson teed off at noon, paired with Kirk Triplett. They found the golf course had become mean overnight.

Sunny skies and a moderate wind had toughened Olympia Fields. Shots played with medium irons rolled instead of braking quickly on the firmer greens, drives ran on and on, and the wind had to be considered. Those conditions, combined with the tension of the last round of the Open, sent scores climbing.

Only six men shot in the 60s, none of them with any hope of winning. Marco Dawson, who began the day tied for 61st place, shot 69 and advanced to a tie for 48th. Peter Lonard, who began tied for

Fourth Round

Kenny Perry (279) shot 67 and tied for third place.

Fourth Round

Jim Furyk	67 - 66 - 67 - 72 – 272	-8
Stephen Leaney	67 - 68 - 68 - 72 – 275	-5
Kenny Perry	72 - 71 - 69 - 67 – 279	-1
Mike Weir	73 - 67 - 68 - 71 – 279	-1
Justin Rose	70 - 71 - 70 - 69 – 280	E
Fredrik Jacobson	69 - 67 - 73 - 71 – 280	E
David Toms	72 - 67 - 70 - 71 – 280	E
Ernie Els	69 - 70 - 69 - 72 – 280	E
Nick Price	71 - 65 - 69 - 75 – 280	E

50th, and Harrington, tied for 39th, both shot 68, and Justin Rose, tied for 24th, and Jonathan Kaye, tied for 33rd, shot 69.

Rose moved up to a tie for fifth, alongside Ernie Els, David Toms, Fredrik Jacobson and Price, all at 280. Harrington and Kaye shared 10th at 281 with Cliff Kresge, Scott Verplank and Billy Mayfair.

Nor did Woods have much hope, but, as ever, he tried. A birdie at the first hole set up a good start, but he needed more. Another at the sixth helped, but even this early in the round the holes were running out. It ended at the ninth, where, in front of a packed grandstand, he took four putts from the edge of the green and double-bogeyed. Three putts at the 10th and he bogeyed again. With another lost stroke at the 11th, he had dropped four strokes in three holes and sunk from sight.

Woods had played the last two rounds in 75 and 72, 147 strokes, one stroke higher than his last two rounds at Muirfield in the 2002 British Open. But he had an excuse there; he had played through horrible weather in the third round and shot 81, then fought back the next day with a closing 65, not good enough, but it showed what he might do.

Here at Olympia Fields, he could do nothing but try. His loyal gallery stuck with him and applauded as, dejected, he walked off the final green.

Dicky Pride played even worse. Tied for fifth going into the last round, Pride had played exceptionally well over the previous two rounds, but his

Nick Price (280) had dropped out of contention by the time he reached the second nine.

game collapsed under the pressure of the Open's last day. Where he had shot 66 in the third round, he soared to 78 in the last and dropped out of sight, finishing tied for 28th.

Ian Leggatt began the day at 206, within six strokes of first place, and shot 77, and Mark Calcavecchia started at 207 but closed with 76.

Hardly anyone had noticed Pride and Leggatt fall behind, but when both Price and Singh began playing like 10-handicappers, the whole crowd wondered what had happened.

Always a reliable driver but chancy putter, Price couldn't keep the ball in play, and for once Singh's elegant swing failed him. Price fell apart from the start, opening with three bogeys, and Singh took a double-bogey 6 at the third with shoddy work from tee to green.

After driving into the right rough in such a position he could do no more than pitch out for a clear shot at the flagstick, Singh dumped his pitch into the right greenside bunker, flew his recovery

Tiger Woods (283) finished 11 strokes off the lead.

Fourth Round

Mike Weir (279) was near the top again.

onto the back collar of the green, left his first putt short, then holed out to save the 6.

Price played it almost as badly, although he did hit the green with his second shot, but with the hole cut toward the right rear, he played his approach to the left rear, in three-putt territory. He, of course, three-putted.

Both men went out in 40, improved slightly coming back, but by then they no longer mattered. Playing such poor golf that it had become funny, they couldn't help laughing. With their collapse, and no one else within range playing decently, the Open was left to Furyk and Leaney.

Throughout the week, Leaney had insisted he felt he could win, even though he had played in only the 1999 championship. He shot 76-72 at Pinehurst and missed the cut.

Paired with Furyk as the last men off the tee Sunday afternoon, Leaney played erratic golf through the first nine. He drove into a fairway bunker at the first hole, took three more shots to reach

Vijay Singh (283) fell from a tie for third to 20th.

the green and bogeyed. Then, in quick order, he birdied the second, bogeyed the third and birdied the fourth. It had taken him four strokes to reach the first green and three to reach the third, not the kind of golf that would win championships.

Furyk, meanwhile, opened with a par 5 at the first hole, but struggled to save par at the second, where he hit his first two shots into the rough and played a 30-yard pitch to the collar of the green, perhaps 20 feet from the hole. Furyk holed it for a par 4 when something worse seemed likely.

"That was huge," his caddie said later. It saved what could have been a two-stroke swing, since Leaney birdied. As it was, Leaney had cut Furyk's lead back to three strokes, where they had begun the day.

Furyk played another key shot at the fifth, where he drove into the left rough, pitched short of the green in the right rough, pitched on and holed a six-foot putt for the par 4 to keep his lead over Leaney at three strokes.

By then, with the rest of the field falling

Spectators, many arriving by train, filled Olympia Fields.

Justin Rose (280) posted four steady rounds.

Jonathan Kaye (281) finally broke par with 69.

Fourth Round

Stephen Leaney (275) took 4 at the 17th, his sixth bogey.

behind, they had gone into a match-play mode, and Leaney battled to cut into Furyk's lead, figuring that if he could hold the honor, Furyk would feel the pressure. The plan didn't work because Leaney couldn't hold the honor. Both men birdied the vulnerable sixth, but now Leaney stumbled.

Playing a 5-iron to the deceptive seventh, he let the shot get away from him. The ball started off to the right, missed the green and buried itself close to the lip of the left greenside bunker. Facing an almost impossible shot, Leaney flailed at the ball, dug it out and winced as it scooted across the green and off the other side, nearly toppling into another bunker. His recovery ran about six feet past the hole, and he ran it in for a very good bogey.

Not learning his lesson, now Leaney pushed his approach to the eighth into the right greenside bunker again and bogeyed once more.

While Leaney tossed strokes away, Furyk had kept rolling up the pars and stepped onto the ninth tee with a comfortable lead — five ahead with just 10 holes to play.

Leaney cut the margin to four when Furyk dropped a stroke at the 10th, but he gave it back at the 11th, where he missed a makeable putt for a par after a woman stripped off her shirt, walked onto the green and tried to give Furyk a flower. Furyk turned away, but the incident clearly upset Leaney's focus.

Quickly, though, Furyk gave back the stroke at the 12th, and after they both parred the 13th, he played a marvelous approach to the 14th that braked within a yard of the hole for a certain birdie. Even though Leaney birdied as well, the holes had run out. He had no hope of catching up.

Now Furyk could concentrate on the 72-hole record. He stood at even par, and even par would beat the record by two strokes.

One stroke slipped away when he bogeyed the 17th, but he could still do it with a par 4 at the 18th.

Taking no chances of throwing away the championship by thinking of the record, Furyk drove with an iron and his approach landed back and left of the hole. An aggressive first putt almost

Fredrik Jacobson (280) shared fifth place.

Peter Lonard (283) finished with 68.

Cliff Kresge (281) climbed into the top 10.

David Toms (280) was even par after 71.

Scott Verplank (281) had started with 76.

Fourth Round

Ernie Els (280) had 72 to finish.

Billy Mayfair (281) had four bogeys in the last nine.

went in, but finished seven feet past. Furyk missed the comeback putt on the high side and tapped in for a 5.

He had finished with two bogeys, and with a final round of 72, two over par, he did no more than match the record of 272.

But he had won the U.S. Open Championship.

Later, after he had been handed the trophy, he embraced his father, Mike Furyk, a club professional who had refused to tinker with his son's peculiar method, cuddled his baby daughter and hugged both his wife, Tabitha, and mother, Linda.

After the cheering had died away and the gallery had headed homeward, and he had time to reflect on the day, he talked about that approach to the 14th. He said that as soon as he laid the club against the ball, "I thought it was the perfect golf shot." Certainly, it wasn't bad, but then he'd thought he had played the perfect shot two holes earlier.

"I thought the best shot of the day was the sec-

Padraig Harrington (281) shot 68 to rise from 39th.

Although finishing with his second consecutive bogey, Furyk tied the 72-hole scoring record and won by three strokes.

ond shot on the 12th. I rifled a 5-iron right at the stick. I was licking my chops and thinking about how good a shot it was, and it landed four yards short of the green and ended up 40 yards from the hole. So I went from playing my best shot of the day to struggling to make a bogey."

He didn't make many, just 10 in four rounds, and only one of those on the first nine. He owned the sixth hole and made a down-payment on the fifth. He played the two of them a combined eight times, and finished six under par. He birdied the fifth twice and the sixth every time he saw it. He made his bogeys on the second nine, two each at the 10th, 12th, 17th and 18th.

Through the week he hit 39 of the 56 fairways on driving holes, and 53 of 72 greens. He had been hurt by the second nine in the opening round, which was the first nine he played, where he had hit only three greens.

But what did all that matter? It mattered only that he had scored low enough to become the national champion.

Furyk's victory march up the 18th fairway had been preceded by another poignant moment. A few hours earlier, Tom Watson and Bruce Edwards, his stricken caddie, had walked up the 18th fairway together once again.

As they approached the green, the crowd lining the ropes began to applaud. Soon the fans seated in the grandstands behind and alongside the green rose and joined in.

When Watson's last putt fell, he bent over, took his ball from the hole, wrapped his arm around Edwards, and the two of them walked off, smiling and waving to the fans as they disappeared into the evening.

It had been such a haunting moment, the clapping and cheering seemed to carry into the night.

103rd U.S. OPEN
The Champion

When a college golf coach on a recruiting mission who watched Jim Furyk play in the Pennsylvania high school championship said he couldn't wait to work on that swing, he lost the sale; no one was going to change the way Furyk swings the golf club.

His career as a professional golfer confirms that he had been right all those years ago, especially now that he reigns as the United States Open champion. Quirky though it is, that swing works.

It works so well, in fact, that during four tense rounds in the Open, Furyk hit 69.6 percent of the fairways (39 of 56) and 73.6 percent of the greens (53 of 72). Over 72 holes at Olympia Fields in 2003, no one did better than Furyk.

No one can deny that Furyk's swing is indeed unorthodox. It has more moving parts than a 12-cylinder Jaguar. But when the Jag is tuned properly, it purrs. Likewise, when Furyk's swing slides into its groove, the result is worth watching.

Furyk takes the club back a little outside the line, then once at the top, he twirls the club in a loop, and when he whips it down, it slips into just the right plane, and Jim delivers a powerful and accurate blow. It's not pretty, and not one you would expect from a player whose father was a golf professional.

Mike Furyk never tampered with his son's swing. He did suggest, however, that he putt with a cross-handed grip, but only after advice from both Arnold Palmer and Gary Player. When Mike asked if they regretted anything about the way they had played the game, they both admitted that, if they could start again, they would both place their left hand below their right on the putter grip. According to Mike Furyk, Palmer claimed, "It's a better stroke."

It certainly did all right by Furyk. Over a 10-year PGA Tour career, Furyk had won seven tournaments, three of them in Las Vegas. He had also won the 2001 Mercedes Championship, the opening event of the season, reserved for tournament winners of the previous year, and the 2002 Memorial Tournament, where Jack Nicklaus plays host.

He has now won at least one tournament in six consecutive seasons and built a reputation for consistency. He's been nicknamed T-4, for all the times he has tied for fourth place, twice during 2003. He had picked good ones — The Players Championship and the Masters.

That reliability had turned him into a money-making machine. Coming in to Olympia Fields, he had placed among the 10 leading scorers in 10 events, more than anyone else, including Tiger Woods. Six years earlier, in 1997, he had set a PGA Tour record by earning $1.6 million without winning a tournament, his last season without at least one first-place finish. Vijay Singh raised it to $3.4 million in 2001.

Leading up to the Open, Furyk had played in 14 tournaments for the year and earned a little over $2.3 million without a victory. The Open added $1,080,000 more, raising his total 2003 earnings to $3.4 million.

Standing 6-foot-2 and weighing 185 pounds, Furyk had grown into a balding 33-year-old by the time he had become the Open champion. He'd been born in West Chester, Pa., not far from Philadelphia, and attended high school in Manheim, in the Amish country, about two hours from the city.

His grip on the U.S. Open trophy proved that Jim Furyk has a swing that works.

The Champion

Many hours in bunkers as a youth prepared Furyk for Olympia Fields.

An accomplished high school athlete, Furyk played quarterback on the football team, point guard in basketball and caught for the baseball team. At the same time, he did well in academics, earning mainly As and Bs.

He turned away from team sports eventually and turned to golf, reasoning to his father that, "In golf you're either the hero or the goat, and I can handle both."

Once committed, he worked hard at his game. He especially remembers a day at the Media Heights Golf Club, near Lancaster, where, just 16 years old, he held a junior membership.

Furyk had planted himself in a bunker at the ninth, working to improve his technique. A group about to tee off watched as they waited, and when they came up the ninth fairway they saw him still blasting away. He was still there when they teed off at the 10th, and when they reached the final hole, they looked over from the 18th green and there he was, still spraying sand, working on that one shot.

"I know the course superintendent wanted to wring my neck a few times," Furyk remembers. "I'd hit putts and wear holes from practicing from the same spot.

"Media Heights was a great club to join for dirt cheap. It was a relatively short course, but you had to manage your game well to play it. For the last couple of years of high school, I played a lot there; it was a great place to practice."

Furyk broke into competitive golf in junior tournaments, and learned quickly that he was on his own.

Mike Furyk had made a deal with his son. He would take him to tournaments, but, he said, "I won't really follow you, because golf has a lot of pressure, and all I can do is add to that pressure by being there." He added that he could do nothing to help; Jim would have to do it all himself.

One day, at a tournament in Kentucky, Jim asked Mike to walk with him.

The second hole was a par 5, Mike remembers. Jim played a nice drive, then hit his second shot into the rough. Immediately he turned and looked at Mike.

"After he finished the hole," Mike remembers, "I said to him, 'If you think you're going to play the game and never hit a bad shot, you might as well quit right now. I know you're trying harder than anyone out here, and that's good enough for me. The next time you hit a bad shot and look for me, I'm not coming out again.'

"He never looked for me again. He understood that whatever he did, I was satisfied."

Perhaps those days drew father and son so closely together that on the morning of the Open's last day, Jim grew so emotional he couldn't wish Mike a happy Father's Day. He choked up. He finally overcame his feelings and gushed it out before the prize ceremony, where, as the gallery watched, he planted a kiss on his father's cheek.

Furyk publicly thanked his father.

After high school, Furyk went on to the University of Arizona, where he played so well he was chosen All-America twice, and then on to professional golf, where, first, he played two years on the Buy.Com Tour, then moved on to the regular PGA Tour for the 1994 season.

He played in his first U.S. Open that year, shot 292 at Oakmont, and tied for 28th place. The next two years he tied for fifth at both Oakland Hills and Congressional.

From 1998 on, though, he dropped further and further behind, until at Bethpage in 2002, he missed the cut for the first time.

Through it all his peculiar swing drew attention. It had been described in many ways, such as like an octopus falling from a tree, but what works, works.

Golf is a game of individual methods; everyone mustn't swing like the great woman golfer Mickey Wright, a model of classic perfection. Nor could they; some just can't do it.

Look at some of the great ones.

Bob Jones, who may have been the best who ever played the game, looped his club at the top, although not so pronounced as Furyk, and it worked for him. Over an eight-year period he won four U.S. Opens and three British Opens, along with five U.S. Amateurs and one British Amateur.

Jack Nicklaus had that flying right elbow, and he didn't hit it badly. Ben Hogan whipped his club back and down through the ball so fast that when he and Sam Snead played together, Snead wouldn't watch, afraid that Hogan's furious lash would upset his own smooth tempo.

Nor was Lee Trevino's a swing to copy. In his prime years, the British writer Leonard Crawley had played first-class amateur golf, good enough to win places on three Walker Cup teams. His own swing had been a model of tempo and precise delivery of clubhead against ball. Writing in London's *Daily Telegraph* after watching Trevino win the 1968 Open, Crawley scoffed at Trevino's action and called it "his agricultural method."

Peculiar? Yes. Effective? Yes indeed. Although not the longest driver in the game, Trevino had been the most accurate of his time. And once he drew his irons, he played shots hardly anyone else could imagine.

As the old saying goes, it's not how but how many.

103rd U.S. OPEN
Olympia Fields Country Club

June 12-15, 2003, Olympia Fields Country Club (North Course), Olympia Fields, Ill.

Rd. 1	Rd. 2	Rd. 3	Rd. 4	Contestant	Rounds				Total	Prize
T5	T1	1	1	Jim Furyk	67	66	67	72	272	$1,080,000.00
T5	T3	2	2	Stephen Leaney	67	68	68	72	275	650,000.00
T57	T54	T33	T3	Kenny Perry	72	71	69	67	279	341,367.00
T81	T27	T12	T3	Mike Weir	73	67	68	71	279	341,367.00
T25	T40	T24	T5	Justin Rose	70	71	70	69	280	185,934.00
T10	T5	T15	T5	Fredrik Jacobson	69	67	73	71	280	185,934.00
T57	T18	T15	T5	David Toms	72	67	70	71	280	185,934.00
T10	T18	T12	T5	Ernie Els	69	70	69	72	280	185,934.00
T45	T5	T3	T5	Nick Price	71	65	69	75	280	185,934.00
T10	T40	T39	T10	Padraig Harrington	69	72	72	68	281	124,936.00
T25	T27	T33	T10	Jonathan Kaye	70	70	72	69	281	124,936.00
T10	T18	T24	T10	Cliff Kresge	69	70	72	70	281	124,936.00
T125	T54	T24	T10	Scott Verplank	76	67	68	70	281	124,936.00
T10	T27	T9	T10	Billy Mayfair	69	71	67	74	281	124,936.00
T10	T27	T24	T15	Hidemichi Tanaka	69	71	71	71	282	93,359.00
T10	T12	T15	T15	Tom Byrum	69	69	71	73	282	93,359.00
T10	T18	T15	T15	Tim Petrovic	69	70	70	73	282	93,359.00
T10	T3	T5	T15	Jonathan Byrd	69	66	71	76	282	93,359.00
T25	T5	T5	T15	Eduardo Romero	70	66	70	76	282	93,359.00
T57	T40	T50	T20	Peter Lonard	72	69	74	68	283	64,170.00
T25	T5	T24	T20	Tiger Woods	70	66	75	72	283	64,170.00
T10	T10	T20	T20	Robert Damron	69	68	73	73	283	64,170.00
T57	T40	T20	T20	Jay Williamson	72	69	69	73	283	64,170.00
T3	T5	T12	T20	Justin Leonard	66	70	72	75	283	64,170.00
T7	T27	T9	T20	Mark Calcavecchia	68	72	67	76	283	64,170.00
T7	T12	T5	T20	Ian Leggatt	68	70	68	77	283	64,170.00
T25	T1	T3	T20	Vijay Singh	70	63	72	78	283	64,170.00
T57	T46	T42	T28	John Maginnes	72	70	72	70	284	41,254.00
T45	T46	T42	T28	Kevin Sutherland	71	71	72	70	284	41,254.00
T1	T10	T33	T28	Tom Watson	65	72	75	72	284	41,254.00
T45	T18	T33	T28	Kirk Triplett	71	68	73	72	284	41,254.00
T25	T12	T20	T28	Stewart Cink	70	68	72	74	284	41,254.00
T1	T18	T20	T28	Brett Quigley	65	74	71	74	284	41,254.00
T45	T27	T5	T28	Dicky Pride	71	69	66	78	284	41,254.00
T25	T12	T42	T35	Brandt Jobe	70	68	76	71	285	32,552.00
T10	T54	T42	T35	Sergio Garcia	69	74	71	71	285	32,552.00
T57	T54	T42	T35	Chris DiMarco	72	71	71	71	285	32,552.00
T25	T54	T42	T35	Fred Funk	70	73	71	71	285	32,552.00
T57	T27	T39	T35	Angel Cabrera	72	68	73	72	285	32,552.00
T25	T27	T15	T35	Chad Campbell	70	70	69	76	285	32,552.00
T57	T27	T9	T35	Mark O'Meara	72	68	67	78	285	32,552.00
T45	T54	T55	T42	Retief Goosen	71	72	73	70	286	25,002.00
T10	T40	T50	T42	Loren Roberts	69	72	74	71	286	25,002.00
T10	T54	T42	T42	Colin Montgomerie	69	74	71	72	286	25,002.00
T25	T27	T39	T42	Bernhard Langer	70	70	73	73	286	25,002.00

103rd U.S. Open

Rd. 1	Rd. 2	Rd. 3	Rd. 4	Contestant	Rounds				Total	Prize
T25	T46	T33	T42	Steve Lowery	70	72	70	74	286	25,002.00
T25	T18	T24	T42	Darren Clarke	70	69	72	75	286	25,002.00
T57	T54	T61	T48	Marco Dawson	72	71	75	69	287	19,025.00
T108	T54	T55	T48	Niclas Fasth	75	68	73	71	287	19,025.00
T92	T12	T42	T48	Woody Austin	74	64	76	73	287	19,025.00
T45	T12	T24	T48	Dan Forsman	71	67	73	76	287	19,025.00
T45	T18	T24	T48	Darron Stiles	71	68	72	76	287	19,025.00
T25	T54	T58	T53	Charles Howell III	70	73	74	71	288	17,004.00
T81	T54	T24	T53	John Rollins	73	70	68	77	288	17,004.00
T25	T27	T50	T55	Phil Mickelson	70	70	75	74	289	16,199.00
T57	T27	T33	T55	Lee Janzen	72	68	72	77	289	16,199.00
T10	T46	T63	T57	Len Mattiace	69	73	77	71	290	15,643.00
T92	T40	T58	T57	*Trip Kuehne	74	67	76	73	290	Medal
T45	T46	T66	T59	*Ricky Barnes	71	71	79	70	291	
T57	T46	T55	T59	Olin Browne	72	70	74	75	291	15,347.00
T57	T46	65	T61	Chris Anderson	72	70	78	72	292	14,810.00
T45	T54	T58	T61	Brian Davis	71	72	74	75	292	14,810.00
T81	T18	T50	T61	Alex Cejka	73	66	76	77	292	14,810.00
T25	T54	68	T64	J.P. Hayes	70	73	79	71	293	14,200.00
T3	T54	T61	T64	Jay Don Blake	66	77	75	75	293	14,200.00
T125	T54	T63	T66	Brian Henninger	76	67	76	76	295	13,711.00
T25	T46	T50	T66	Fred Couples	70	72	73	80	295	13,711.00
T57	T27	T66	68	Ryan Dillon	72	68	81	80	301	13,334.00

Tim Clark	69	75	144	Bryce Molder	74	72	146	Kent Jones	76	73	149
Steve Flesch	73	71	144	Dean Wilson	76	70	146	* Luke List	75	74	149
Jose Maria Olazabal	74	70	144	Robert Allenby	75	71	146	Tommy Armour III	76	73	149
Tom Gillis	68	76	144	David Smail	74	72	146	Sean Murphy	78	71	149
Rob Bradley	73	71	144	* Chris Baryla	72	74	146	Billy Andrade	78	72	150
Joe Durant	72	72	144	Jerry Kelly	75	72	147	Nick Faldo	75	75	150
Stuart Appleby	75	69	144	Bob Estes	70	77	147	David Duval	78	72	150
Neal Lancaster	72	72	144	Doug Dunakey	73	74	147	Rich Beem	74	76	150
Craig Parry	70	74	144	Toru Taniguchi	79	68	147	Brad Faxon	73	77	150
Adam Scott	72	72	144	Bob Tway	74	73	147	Davis Love III	76	75	151
Spike McRoy	71	73	144	Sean McCarty	78	69	147	Matt Seppanen	76	76	152
Joe Ogilvie	70	74	144	Jay Haas	75	72	147	* Rick Reinsberg	76	76	152
Dudley Hart	72	73	145	Bill Lunde	74	73	147	Steve Gotsche	76	76	152
Paul Casey	76	69	145	Rocco Mediate	73	74	147	* Chez Reavie	75	78	153
Richard Johnson	71	74	145	Doug Labelle II	72	76	148	Alan Morin	79	74	153
Geoff Ogilvy	74	71	145	Warren Schutte	77	71	148	Scott McCarron	74	79	153
Craig Bowden	76	69	145	Corey Pavin	72	76	148	Cortney Brisson	75	78	153
Jeff Sluman	74	71	145	Tom Kite	72	76	148	Anthony Arvidson	75	78	153
Jesper Parnevik	74	71	145	Shigeki Maruyama	75	73	148	K.J. Choi	79	74	153
Thomas Bjorn	71	74	145	Mark Wurtz	76	72	148	Chris Smith	77	77	154
* John Bradley Holmes	76	69	145	Larry Mize	76	72	148	Michael Campbell	74	80	154
Geoffrey Sisk	76	70	146	Bret Guetz	75	73	148	Greg Hiller	78	77	155
Grant Waite	74	72	146	Chris Riley	76	72	148	Jason Knutzon	75	81	156
Jeff Maggert	74	72	146	Rory Sabbatini	73	75	148	Joey Sindelar	76	81	157
Roland Thatcher	73	73	146	Maarten Lafeber	75	73	148	Don Pooley	81	76	157
Hiroshi Matsuo	72	74	146	Paul Lawrie	75	74	149	Roy Biancalana	75	84	159
Trevor Immelman	72	74	146	Bob Burns	78	71	149	* Tom Glissmeyer	80	79	159
* Hunter Mahan	74	72	146	* Bill Haas	73	76	149	Hale Irwin			WD
Brian Gay	77	69	146	Brad Elder	75	74	149				
Scott Hoch	70	76	146	Rod Pampling	72	77	149				

Professionals not returning 72-hole scores received $1,000 each.

*Denotes amateur.

103rd U.S. OPEN Statistics

Hole	1	2	3	4	5	6	7	8	9	10	11	12	13	14	15	16	17	18	Total	
Par	5	4	4	3	4	5	3	4	4	4	4	4	4	4	3	4	3	4	70	
Jim Furyk																				
Round 1	④	③	③	3	③	④	[4]	4	③	4	③	[5]	4	[5]	3	4	3	[5]	67	
Round 2	④	4	4	3	4	④	3	4	4	4	4	4	③	③	3	4	3	4	66	
Round 3	5	4	4	3	③	④	3	4	③	[5]	4	4	4	4	②	4	[4]	③	67	
Round 4	5	4	4	3	4	④	3	4	4	[5]	4	[5]	4	③	3	4	[4]	[5]	72	272
Stephen Leaney																				
Round 1	5	4	4	3	4	④	3	4	4	4	4	[5]	③	4	②	4	②	4	67	
Round 2	④	4	4	3	4	5	3	4	4	4	4	4	4	4	3	4	3	③	68	
Round 3	④	4	4	3	③	5	3	4	③	[6]	[5]	4	4	4	②	4	3	③	68	
Round 4	[6]	③	[5]	②	4	④	[4]	[5]	4	4	[5]	4	③	4	3	4	[4]	4	72	275
Kenny Perry																				
Round 1	④	③	4	3	4	5	3	4	4	[5]	4	4	[5]	4	3	4	[4]	[5]	72	
Round 2	[6]	[5]	4	3	4	④	3	③	[5]	③	[5]	4	[5]	③	3	4	3	4	71	
Round 3	5	4	4	3	③	5	[4]	4	4	4	[5]	[5]	4	③	②	4	3	③	69	
Round 4	④	③	③	3	[5]	④	3	4	4	4	4	4	4	[5]	3	③	3	4	67	279
Mike Weir																				
Round 1	5	4	4	3	4	④	3	[6]	[6]	[5]	4	4	4	③	3	4	3	4	73	
Round 2	[7]	4	4	3	③	5	3	③	4	4	4	4	4	③	②	③	3	4	67	
Round 3	5	③	4	3	4	③	3	4	③	4	4	4	4	[5]	3	[5]	3	4	68	
Round 4	5	4	4	3	4	5	②	4	[5]	4	4	4	4	③	3	4	[4]	[5]	71	279

◯ Circled numbers represent birdies or eagles. ☐ Squared numbers represent bogeys or worse.

Hole	Yards	Par	Eagles	Birdies	Pars	Bogeys	Double Bogeys	Higher	Average
1	576	5	8	111	267	53	6	1	4.868
2	400	4	1	84	280	70	11	0	4.013
3	389	4	0	68	288	80	10	0	4.072
4	164	3	0	70	331	42	3	0	2.951
5	440	4	0	49	248	125	21	3	4.287
6	555	5	13	162	207	53	11	0	4.747
7	212	3	0	37	294	104	8	3	3.206
8	433	4	0	51	259	119	13	4	4.238
9	496	4	0	33	277	118	18	0	4.271
OUT	3,665	36	22	665	2,451	764	101	11	36.653
10	444	4	0	31	279	119	16	1	4.276
11	467	4	0	37	293	108	7	1	4.197
12	458	4	3	33	234	153	20	3	4.365
13	397	4	1	64	276	96	8	1	4.110
14	414	4	0	53	250	124	19	0	4.244
15	187	3	0	67	317	58	4	0	2.998
16	451	4	1	78	283	74	9	1	4.034
17	247	3	0	34	261	137	14	0	3.294
18	460	4	0	44	282	105	12	3	4.211
IN	3,525	34	5	441	2,475	974	109	10	35.729
TOTAL	7,190	70	27	1,106	4,926	1,738	210	21	72.382

U.S. OPEN Past Results

Date	Winner	Score	Runner-Up	Venue
1895	Horace Rawlins	173 - 36 holes	Willie Dunn	Newport GC, Newport, R.I.
1896	James Foulis	152 - 36 holes	Horace Rawlins	Shinnecock Hills GC, Southampton, N.Y.
1897	Joe Lloyd	162 - 36 holes	Willie Anderson	Chicago GC, Wheaton, Ill.
1898	Fred Herd	328 - 72 holes	Alex Smith	Myopia Hunt Club, S. Hamilton, Mass.
1899	Willie Smith	315	George Low / Val Fitzjohn / W.H. Way	Baltimore CC, Baltimore, Md.
1900	Harry Vardon	313	J.H. Taylor	Chicago GC, Wheaton, Ill.
1901	*Willie Anderson (85)	331	Alex Smith (86)	Myopia Hunt Club, S. Hamilton, Mass.
1902	Laurie Auchterlonie	307	Stewart Gardner	Garden City GC, Garden City, N.Y.
1903	*Willie Anderson (82)	307	David Brown (84)	Baltusrol GC, Springfield, N.J.
1904	Willie Anderson	303	Gil Nicholls	Glen View Club, Golf, Ill.
1905	Willie Anderson	314	Alex Smith	Myopia Hunt Club, S. Hamilton, Mass.
1906	Alex Smith	295	Willie Smith	Onwentsia Club, Lake Forest, Ill.
1907	Alex Ross	302	Gil Nicholls	Philadelphia Cricket Club, Chestnut Hill, Pa.
1908	*Fred McLeod (77)	322	Willie Smith (83)	Myopia Hunt Club, S. Hamilton, Mass.
1909	George Sargent	290	Tom McNamara	Englewood GC, Englewood, N.J.
1910	*Alex Smith (71)	298	John J. McDermott (75) / Macdonald Smith (77)	Philadelphia Cricket Club, Chestnut Hill, Pa.
1911	*John J. McDermott (80)	307	Michael J. Brady (82) / George O. Simpson (85)	Chicago GC, Wheaton, Ill.
1912	John J. McDermott	294	Tom McNamara	CC of Buffalo, Buffalo, N.Y.
1913	*Francis Ouimet (72)	304	Harry Vardon (77) / Edward Ray (78)	The Country Club, Brookline, Mass.
1914	Walter Hagen	290	Charles Evans Jr.	Midlothian CC, Blue Island, Ill.
1915	Jerome D. Travers	297	Tom McNamara	Baltusrol GC, Springfield, N.J.
1916	Charles Evans Jr.	286	Jock Hutchinson	Minikahda Club, Minneapolis, Minn.
1917-18	No Championships Played — World War I			
1919	*Walter Hagen (77)	301	Michael J. Brady (78)	Brae Burn CC, West Newton, Mass.
1920	Edward Ray	295	Harry Vardon / Jack Burke, Sr. / Leo Diegel / Jock Hutchison	Inverness Club, Toledo, Ohio
1921	James M. Barnes	289	Walter Hagen / Fred McLeod	Columbia CC, Chevy Chase, Md.
1922	Gene Sarazen	288	John L. Black / Robert T. Jones Jr.	Skokie CC, Glencoe, Ill.
1923	*Robert T. Jones Jr. (76)	296	Bobby Cruickshank (78)	Inwood CC, Inwood, N.Y.
1924	Cyril Walker	297	Robert T. Jones Jr.	Oakland Hills CC, Birmingham, Mich.
1925	*William Macfarlane (147)	291	Robert T. Jones Jr. (148)	Worcester CC, Worcester, Mass.
1926	Robert T. Jones Jr.	293	Joc Turnesa	Scioto CC, Columbus, Ohio
1927	*Tommy Armour (76)	301	Harry Cooper (79)	Oakmont CC, Oakmont, Pa.
1928	*Johnny Farrell (143)	294	Robert T. Jones Jr. (144)	Olympia Fields CC, Matteson, Ill.

Past Results

Date	Winner	Score	Runner-Up	Venue
1929	*Robert T. Jones Jr. (141)	294	Al Espinosa (164)	Winged Foot GC, Mamaroneck, N.Y.
1930	Robert T. Jones Jr.	287	Macdonald Smith	Interlachen CC, Hopkins, Minn.
1931	*Billy Burke (149-148)	292	George Von Elm (149-149)	Inverness Club, Toledo, Ohio
1932	Gene Sarazen	286	Phil Perkins	Fresh Meadows CC, Flushing, N.Y.
1933	Johnny Goodman	287	Bobby Cruickshank Ralph Guldahl	North Shore CC, Glenview, Ill.
1934	Olin Dutra	293	Gene Sarazen	Merion Cricket Club, Ardmore, Pa.
1935	Sam Parks Jr.	299	Jimmy Thomson	Oakmont CC, Oakmont, Pa.
1936	Tony Manero	282	Harry Cooper	Baltusrol GC, Springfield, N.J.
1937	Ralph Guldahl	281	Sam Snead	Oakland Hills CC, Birmingham, Mich.
1938	Ralph Guldahl	284	Dick Metz	Cherry Hills CC, Englewood, Col.
1939	*Byron Nelson (68-70)	284	Craig Wood (68-73) Denny Shute (76)	Philadelphia CC, West Conshohocken, Pa.
1940	*Lawson Little (70)	287	Gene Sarazen (73)	Canterbury GC, Cleveland, Ohio
1941	Craig Wood	284	Denny Shute	Colonial Club, Fort Worth, Texas
1942-45	No Championships Played — World War II			
1946	*Lloyd Mangrum (72-72)	284	Vic Ghezzi (72-73) Byron Nelson (72-73)	Canterbury GC, Cleveland, Ohio
1947	*Lew Worsham (69)	282	Sam Snead (70)	St. Louis CC, Clayton, Mo.
1948	Ben Hogan	276	Jimmy Demaret	Riviera CC, Los Angeles, Calif.
1949	Cary Middlecoff	286	Sam Snead Clayton Heafner	Medinah CC, Medinah, Ill.
1950	*Ben Hogan (69)	287	Lloyd Mangrum (73) George Fazio (75)	Merion GC, Ardmore, Pa.
1951	Ben Hogan	287	Clayton Heafner	Oakland Hills CC, Birmingham, Mich.
1952	Julius Boros	281	Ed (Porky) Oliver	Northwood CC, Dallas, Texas
1953	Ben Hogan	283	Sam Snead	Oakmont CC, Oakmont, Pa.
1954	Ed Furgol	284	Gene Littler	Baltusrol GC, Springfield, N.J.
1955	*Jack Fleck (69)	287	Ben Hogan (72)	The Olympic Club, San Francisco, Calif.
1956	Cary Middlecoff	281	Ben Hogan Julius Boros	Oak Hill CC, Rochester, N.Y.
1957	*Dick Mayer (72)	282	Cary Middlecoff (79)	Inverness Club, Toledo, Ohio
1958	Tommy Bolt	283	Gary Player	Southern Hills CC, Tulsa, Okla.
1959	Billy Casper	282	Bob Rosburg	Winged Foot GC, Mamaroneck, N.Y.
1960	Arnold Palmer	280	Jack Nicklaus	Cherry Hills CC, Englewood, Col.
1961	Gene Littler	281	Bob Goalby Doug Sanders	Oakland Hills CC, Birmingham, Mich.
1962	*Jack Nicklaus (71)	283	Arnold Palmer (74)	Oakmont CC, Oakmont, Pa.
1963	*Julius Boros (70)	293	Jacky Cupit (73) Arnold Palmer (76)	The Country Club, Brookline, Mass.
1964	Ken Venturi	278	Tommy Jacobs	Congressional CC, Bethesda, Md.
1965	*Gary Player (71)	282	Kel Nagle (74)	Bellerive CC, St. Louis, Mo.
1966	*Billy Casper (69)	278	Arnold Palmer (73)	The Olympic Club, San Francisco, Calif.
1967	Jack Nicklaus	275	Arnold Palmer	Baltusrol GC, Springfield, N.J.
1968	Lee Trevino	275	Jack Nicklaus	Oak Hill CC, Rochester, N.Y.
1969	Orville Moody	281	Deane Beman Al Geiberger Bob Rosburg	Champions GC, Houston, Texas
1970	Tony Jacklin	281	Dave Hill	Hazeltine National GC, Chaska, Minn.
1971	*Lee Trevino (68)	280	Jack Nicklaus (71)	Merion GC, Ardmore, Pa.
1972	Jack Nicklaus	290	Bruce Crampton	Pebble Beach GL, Pebble Beach, Calif.
1973	Johnny Miller	279	John Schlee	Oakmont CC, Oakmont, Pa.

Date	Winner	Score	Runner-Up	Venue
1974	Hale Irwin	287	Forrest Fezler	Winged Foot GC, Mamaroneck, N.Y.
1975	*Lou Graham (71)	287	John Mahaffey (73)	Medinah CC, Medinah, Ill.
1976	Jerry Pate	277	Tom Weiskopf Al Geiberger	Atlanta Athletic Club, Duluth, Ga.
1977	Hubert Green	278	Lou Graham	Southern Hills CC, Tulsa, Okla.
1978	Andy North	285	Dave Stockton J.C. Snead	Cherry Hills CC, Englewood, Col.
1979	Hale Irwin	284	Gary Player Jerry Pate	Inverness Club, Toledo, Ohio
1980	Jack Nicklaus	272	Isao Aoki	Baltusrol GC, Springfield, N.J.
1981	David Graham	273	George Burns Bill Rogers	Merion GC, Ardmore, Pa.
1982	Tom Watson	282	Jack Nicklaus	Pebble Beach GL, Pebble Beach, Calif.
1983	Larry Nelson	280	Tom Watson	Oakmont CC, Oakmont, Pa.
1984	*Fuzzy Zoeller (67)	276	Greg Norman (75)	Winged Foot GC, Mamaroneck, N.Y.
1985	Andy North	279	Dave Barr Chen Tze Chung Denis Watson	Oakland Hills CC, Birmingham, Mich.
1986	Raymond Floyd	279	Lanny Wadkins Chip Beck	Shinnecock Hills GC, Southampton, N.Y.
1987	Scott Simpson	277	Tom Watson	The Olympic Club, San Francisco, Calif.
1988	*Curtis Strange (71)	278	Nick Faldo (75)	The Country Club, Brookline, Mass.
1989	Curtis Strange	278	Chip Beck Mark McCumber Ian Woosnam	Oak Hill CC, Rochester, N.Y.
1990	*Hale Irwin (74+3)	280	Mike Donald (74+4)	Medinah CC, Medinah, Ill.
1991	*Payne Stewart (75)	282	Scott Simpson (77)	Hazeltine National GC, Chaska, Minn.
1992	Tom Kite	285	Jeff Sluman	Pebble Beach GL, Pebble Beach, Calif.
1993	Lee Janzen	272	Payne Stewart	Baltusrol GC, Springfield, N.J.
1994	*Ernie Els (74+4+4)	279	Loren Roberts (74+4+5) Colin Montgomerie (78)	Oakmont CC, Oakmont, Pa.
1995	Corey Pavin	280	Greg Norman	Shinnecock Hills GC, Southampton, N.Y.
1996	Steve Jones	278	Tom Lehman Davis Love III	Oakland Hills CC, Birmingham, Mich.
1997	Ernie Els	276	Colin Montgomerie	Congressional CC, Bethesda, Md.
1998	Lee Janzen	280	Payne Stewart	The Olympic Club, San Francisco, Calif.
1999	Payne Stewart	279	Phil Mickelson	Pinehurst No. 2, Pinehurst, N.C.
2000	Tiger Woods	272	Miguel Angel Jimenez Ernie Els	Pebble Beach GL, Pebble Beach, Calif.
2001	*Retief Goosen (70)	276	Mark Brooks (72)	Southern Hills CC, Tulsa, Okla.
2002	Tiger Woods	277	Phil Mickelson	Bethpage State Park, Farmingdale, N.Y.
2003	Jim Furyk	272	Stephen Leaney	Olympia Fields CC, Olympia Fields, Ill.

*Winner in playoff; figures in parentheses indicate scores

103rd U.S. OPEN Championship Records

Oldest champion (years/months/days)
   45/0/15 — Hale Irwin (1990)

Youngest champion
   19/10/14 — John J. McDermott (1911)

Most victories
   4 — Willie Anderson (1901, '03, '04, '05)
   4 — Robert T. Jones Jr. (1923, '26, '29, '30)
   4 — Ben Hogan (1948, '50, '51, '53)
   4 — Jack Nicklaus (1962, '67, '72, '80)
   3 — Hale Irwin (1974, '79, '90)
   2 — by 15 players: Alex Smith (1906, '10), John J. McDermott (1911, '12), Walter Hagen (1914, '19), Gene Sarazen (1922, '32), Ralph Guldahl (1937, '38), Cary Middlecoff (1949, '56), Julius Boros (1952, '63), Billy Casper (1959, '66), Lee Trevino (1968, '71), Andy North (1978, '85), Curtis Strange (1988, '89), Ernie Els (1994, '97), Lee Janzen (1993, '98), Payne Stewart (1991, '99), and Tiger Woods (2000, '02).

Consecutive victories
   Willie Anderson (1903, '04, '05)
   John J. McDermott (1911, '12)
   Robert T. Jones Jr. (1929, '30)
   Ralph Guldahl (1937, '38)
   Ben Hogan (1950, '51)
   Curtis Strange (1988, '89)

Most times runner-up
   4 — Sam Snead
   4 — Robert T. Jones Jr.
   4 — Arnold Palmer
   4 — Jack Nicklaus

Longest course
   7,214 yards — Bethpage State Park (Black Course), Farmingdale, N.Y. (2002)

Shortest course
   Since World War II
   6,528 yards — Merion GC (East Course), Ardmore, Pa. (1971, '81)

Most often host club of Open
   7 — Baltusrol GC, Springfield, N.J. (1903, '15, '36, '54, '67, '80, '93)
   7 — Oakmont (Pa.) CC (1927, '35, '53, '62, '73, '83, '94)

Largest entry
   8,468 (2002)

Smallest entry
   11 (1895)

Lowest score, 72 holes
   272 — Jack Nicklaus (63-71-70-68), at Baltusrol GC (Lower Course), Springfield, N.J. (1980)
   272 — Lee Janzen (67-67-69-69), at Baltusrol GC (Lower Course), Springfield, N.J. (1993)
   272 — Tiger Woods (65-69-71-67), at Pebble Beach GL, Pebble Beach, Calif. (2000)
   272 — Jim Furyk (67-66-67-72), at Olympia Fields CC (North Course), Olympia Fields, Ill. (2003)

Lowest score, first 54 holes
   200 — Jim Furyk (67-66-67), at Olympia Fields CC (North Course), Olympia Fields, Ill. (2003)

Lowest score, last 54 holes
   203 — Loren Roberts (69-64-70), at Oakmont CC, Oakmont, Pa. (1994)

Lowest score, first 36 holes
   133 — Vijay Singh (70-63), at Olympia Fields CC (North Course), Olympia Fields, Ill. (2003)
   133 — Jim Furyk (67-66), at Olympia Fields CC (North Course), Olympia Fields, Ill. (2003)

Lowest score, last 36 holes
   132 — Larry Nelson (65-67), at Oakmont CC, Oakmont, Pa. (1983)

Lowest score, 9 holes
   29 — Neal Lancaster (second nine, fourth round) at Shinnecock Hills GC, Southampton, N.Y. (1995)
   29 — Neal Lancaster (second nine, second round) at Oakland Hills CC, Birmingham, Mich. (1996)
   29 — Vijay Singh (second nine, second round), at Olympia Fields CC (North Course), Olympia Fields, Ill. (2003)

Lowest score, 18 holes
   63 — Johnny Miller, fourth round at Oakmont CC, Oakmont, Pa. (1973)
   63 — Jack Nicklaus, first round at Baltusrol GC (Lower Course), Springfield, N.J. (1980)
   63 — Tom Weiskopf, first round at Baltusrol GC (Lower Course), Springfield, N.J. (1980)
   63 — Vijay Singh, second round at Olympia Fields CC (North Course), Olympia Fields, Ill. (2003)

Largest winning margin
   15 — Tiger Woods (272), at Pebble Beach GL, Pebble Beach Calif. (2000)

Highest winning score
   Since World War II
   293 — Julius Boros, at The Country Club, Brookline, Mass. (1963) (won in playoff)

Best start by champion
   63 — Jack Nicklaus, at Baltusrol GC (Lower Course), Springfield, N.J. (1980)

Best finish by champion
   63 — Johnny Miller, at Oakmont (Pa.) CC (1973)

Worst start by champion
  Since World War II
  76 — Ben Hogan, at Oakland Hills CC (South Course), Birmingham, Mich. (1951)
  76 — Jack Fleck, at The Olympic Club (Lake Course), San Francisco, Calif. (1955)
Worst finish by champion
  Since World War II
  75 — Cary Middlecoff, at Medinah CC (No. 3 Course), Medinah, Ill. (1949)
  75 — Hale Irwin, at Inverness Club, Toledo, Ohio (1979)
Lowest score to lead field, 18 holes
  63 — Jack Nicklaus and Tom Weiskopf, at Baltusrol GC (Lower Course), Springfield, N.J. (1980)
Lowest score to lead field, 36 holes
  133 — Vijay Singh (70-63) and Jim Furyk (67-66), at Olympia Fields CC (North Course), Olympia Fields, Ill. (2003)
Lowest score to lead field, 54 holes
  200 — Jim Furyk (67-66-67), at Olympia Fields CC (North Course), Olympia Fields, Ill. (2003)
Highest score to lead field, 18 holes
  Since World War II
  71 — Sam Snead, at Oakland Hills CC (South Course), Birmingham, Mich. (1951)
  71 — Tommy Bolt, Julius Boros, and Dick Metz, at Southern Hills CC, Tulsa, Okla. (1958)
  71 — Tony Jacklin, at Hazeltine National GC, Chaska, Minn. (1970)
  71 — Orville Moody, Jack Nicklaus, Chi Chi Rodriguez, Mason Rudolph, Tom Shaw, and Kermit Zarley, at Pebble Beach (Calif.) Golf Links (1972)
Highest score to lead field, 36 holes
  Since World War II
  144 — Bobby Locke (73-71), at Oakland Hills CC (South Course), Birmingham, Mich. (1951)
  144 — Tommy Bolt (67-77) and E. Harvie Ward (74-70), at The Olympic Club (Lake Course), San Francisco, Calif. (1955)
  144 — Homero Blancas (74-70), Bruce Crampton (74-70), Jack Nicklaus (71-73), Cesar Seduno (72-72), Lanny Wadkins (76-68) and Kermit Zarley (71-73), at Pebble Beach (Calif.) Golf Links (1972)
Highest score to lead field, 54 holes
  Since World War II
  218 — Bobby Locke (73-71-74), at Oakland Hills CC (South Course), Birmingham, Mich. (1951)
  218 — Jacky Cupit (70-72-76), at The Country Club, Brookline, Mass. (1963)
Lowest 36-hole cut
  143 — at Olympia Fields CC (North Course), Olympia Fields, Ill. (2003)
Highest 36-hole cut
  155 — at The Olympic Club (Lakeside Course), San Francisco, Calif. (1955)

Most players to tie for lead, 18 holes
  7 — at Pebble Beach (Calif.) Golf Links (1972); at Southern Hills CC, Tulsa, Okla. (1977); and at Shinnecock Hills GC, Southampton, N.Y. (1896)
Most players to tie for lead, 36 holes
  6 — at Pebble Beach (Calif.) Golf Links (1972)
Most players to tie for lead, 54 holes
  4 — at Oakmont (Pa.) CC (1973)
Most sub-par rounds, championship
  124 — at Medinah CC (No. 3 Course), Medinah, Ill. (1990)
Most sub-par 72-hole totals, championship
  28 — at Medinah CC (No. 3 Course), Medinah, Ill. (1990)
Most sub-par scores, first round
  39 — at Medinah CC (No. 3 Course), Medinah, Ill. (1990)
Most sub-par scores, second round
  47 — at Medinah CC (No. 3 Course), Medinah, Ill. (1990)
Most sub-par scores, third round
  24 — at Medinah CC (No. 3 Course), Medinah, Ill. (1990)
Most sub-par scores, fourth round
  18 — at Baltusrol GC (Lower Course), Springfield, N.J. (1993)
Most sub-par rounds by one player in one championship
  4 — Billy Casper, at The Olympic Club (Lakeside Course), San Francisco, Calif. (1966)
  4 — Lee Trevino, at Oak Hill CC (East Course), Rochester, N.Y. (1968)
  4 — Tony Jacklin, at Hazeltine National GC, Chaska, Minn. (1970)
  4 — Lee Janzen, at Baltusrol GC (Lower Course), Springfield, N.J. (1993)
Highest score, one hole
  19 — Ray Ainsley, at the 16th (par 4) at Cherry Hills CC, Englewood, Col. (1938)
Most consecutive birdies
  6 — George Burns (holes 2–7), at Pebble Beach (Calif.) Golf Links (1972) and Andy Dillard (holes 1-6), at Pebble Beach (Calif.) Golf Links (1992)
Most consecutive 3s
  7 — Hubert Green (holes 10–16), at Southern Hills Country Club, Tulsa, Okla. (1977)
  7 — Peter Jacobsen (holes 1–7), at The Country Club, Brookline, Mass. (1988)
Most consecutive Opens
  44 — Jack Nicklaus (1957-2000)
Most Opens completed 72 holes
  35 — Jack Nicklaus
Most consecutive Opens completed 72 holes
  22 — Walter Hagen (1913-36; no Championships 1917-18)
  22 — Gene Sarazen (1920-41)
  22 — Gary Player (1958-79)

Robert Sommers is the former editor and publisher of the USGA's *Golf Journal*, author of *The U.S. Open: Golf's Ultimate Challenge* and *Golf Anecdotes*. He is based in Port St. Lucie, Fla.

Michael Cohen is a photographer based in New York City and a contributor to many magazines and books.

Phil Inglis is a photographer based in England and a contributor to many publications.